LIFE UPON THE
WICKED STAGE

A Sociological Study of Entertainers

Jacqueline Boles

iUniverse, Inc.
New York Bloomington

Life upon the Wicked Stage
A Sociological Study of Entertainers

iUniverse books may be ordered through booksellers or by contacting:

iUniverse
1663 Liberty Drive
Bloomington, IN 47403
www.iuniverse.com
1-800-Authors (1-800-288-4677)

ISBN: 978-1-4502-3151-0 (pbk)
ISBN: 978-1-4502-3152-7 (cloth)
ISBN: 978-1-4502-3153-4 (ebk)

Printed in the United States of America

iUniverse rev. date: 7/16/2010

DEDICATION

For Rex Dane, aka Don Boles: husband, father, magician, piano tuner, author, wood turner, mentalist, violinist and monologist. You are much loved and much missed.

CONTENTS

FOREWARD

Alive, Alive on the inside! This phrase has announced carnival sideshows for several hundred years. The outside talker (barker) gathers a tip (crowd) to view the magicians, sword swallowers, snake handlers, fire eaters and "human oddities" who will perform inside the tent. "For just 25cents, a quarter of a dollar you can see ten acts, count 'em, ten acts, all alive on the inside." Thousands of show people have gotten their start playing carnivals, medicine shows, and other traveling road shows. I grew up on a carnival. When I became an academic, my colleague and friend, Marcello Truzzi, and I wrote about carnivals and outdoor show business.

Marcello and I first met Jackie Boles when she was presenting a paper at the national meeting of the **American Sociological Association** in 1974. Jackie's husband, Don, had played carnivals; they performed a mind reading act, and Jackie's dissertation was on strippers. I knew I had met a kindred spirit.

Jackie has written this book about show people, not just carnies, but those who perform "alive, alive" on the inside and out. With a few important exceptions, we sociologists have neglected show business as an arena of investigation. In spite of the fact that it is such an important segment of our economy and our culture, show business and show people are rarely subjects of academic study.

In this study Jackie presents an academic (but jargon free) portrait of live performers. She seeks to identify the commonalities among those who perform before audiences. Though some self-important entertainers might object, the stresses endured and the joys experienced by carnies, strippers, singers and stand-up comics are similar. In this study the reader will discover the paths by which show business greats as well as those who are small-time, "benny-bit-parts" find their way to the stage. This study makes an important contribution to the sociological understanding of the culture industry and is also "alive, alive, on the inside."

Patrick Easto
Eastern Michigan University

ACKNOWLEDGMENTS

For me this book has been a labor of love. I have known several of the people profiled and have listened to the stories of countless entertainers not profiled, e.g., Morgana the Wild One, Sally Rand, Burt Lancaster, Tom Mullica and Peter Rich plus countless magicians, comics, and outdoor showfolks. So many of them have so generously shared their experiences with me.

I have profited from the support of several sociologists, most especially Pat Easto, Muriel Cantor, Marcello Truzzi, Al Garbin, Clifton Bryant and Miriam Boeri. Several graduate students helped me, especially Paula Moore, and Paul Jean. I appreciate the support of the American Sociological Society's Fund for the Advancement of the Discipline program. All my colleagues at Georgia State University have been supportive beyond all reason. Special thanks go to Michael Motes (entertainment editor of the *Atlanta Journal*) and Shirley Thomas, dancer and friend.

The inspiration for this book was, of course, Rex Dane. When he was a teen, he wanted to be a strolling violinist; later he was a mind reader. Over the years we played sideshows and he continued to perform "live" as a magician and monologist. He wrote several "classics" of outdoor show business, including *Midway Magic*, *The Midway Showman*, and the *Complete Pitchman*. Rex Dane and assistant never made it to the big time, but as Sally Rand told me, "Show business is a tough life, a hard life, but I would have no other."

INTRODUCTION

When my husband and I married in 1953, we played movie theaters around the Southeast with a spook show and mind reading act. My husband's stage name was Rex Dane. In the theater lobby we had a fish bowl, stacks of white 2 by 4 cards, pencils and a sign that read, "Ask Rex Dane a question. Write your question, place your initials on your card, fold it twice and place it in the fish bowl." Most questions were like, "Does Bill really love me?" At the start of his show Rex Dane drew a card from the fish bowl, placed it to his forehead and asked, "Is there a DB in the audience?" When DB responded, my husband said, "Was your question, does Bill really love me?" Then my husband responded, "Yes, DB, Bill does really love you, but he is shy. You will have to be patient and encourage him." Then Rex Dane would proceed to the next question. I was the essential but silent partner (For an extended description of the act, see Boles 1996).

On Saturday night we put on a spook show. We rented a hearse which was parked in front of the theater; then we showed a couple of horror movies. Our live show began about eleven. We used magic illusions that had a "spooky" flavor and then at midnight, the ghosts and goblins (created by phosphorescent paint on pieces of wood) ran through the theater. This was show business, albeit very small-time.

Today show business is a multimillion dollar business, and its celebrities and sports figures are the most famous people on earth. Yet, most entertainers are neither rich nor famous. As a sociologist and an ex-entertainer, I have wondered why so many people persist in the business in spite of the high rate of failure, disappointment and rejection. Most entertainers are unemployed most of the time. They play one night stands for less than they could make waiting tables. Yet, unlike Rex Dane and partner, they persist. This is a book about entertainers: their family backgrounds, reasons for choosing entertainment and career patterns. I hope that the data from this study both contribute to our understanding of professional live performers and also to the study of the culture industry.

Show people are defined as those who perform before live audiences during their entire careers. Even though many in the sample (Jack Benny, Tupac Shakur) performed in a variety of venues and media, they continued to work "live" during their careers. The entertainer, in contrast to the person whose entire career is in film or television, takes sustenance from live audiences and is as addicted to audience response as a junkie is to his fix. All of the entertainers are drawn from popular and mass culture; performers in the "arts" have been excluded as the art world is organized differently than popular culture. Further, the reference group for those in the arts includes critics who are generally of little importance to popular artists.

Popular entertainers can be classified into five groupings: musicians, singers, dancers, comics and variety artists, e.g., magicians, jugglers, mimes, etc., acting is a fundamental component of each. These five specialities have persisted from the beginning of live performance until the present.

The data are based on a content analysis of a probability sample of 117 biographies and autobiographies of American show people. The biographies are listed in Appendix A. In the text quotations from the biographies are not identified by author if the book is in the appendix.

Scholars in the humanities have reported on various types of venues, e.g., the circus, vaudeville, showboats, and the like. An ever-expanding number of biographies and autobiographies of entertainers populate bookstores and web pages; successful musicians and singers are particularly well represented. However, social scientists have shown scant interest in entertainment or entertainers.

Research on entertainers usually derives from one of two theoretical directions.

Entertainer as deviant. Professional performers have most often been identified as deviants by both the general public and by social scientists. Alan Merriam (1964), the musicologist, said that musicians could be characterized as having low status, high importance and the capitalization of their deviant status. The attribution of deviance to entertainers is the result of their status as stranger, the ultimate outsider. Simmel (1971:145) characterized the stranger as ". . . not bound up originally to members of the host society through established ties of kinship, locality or occupation." The stranger and/ or sojourner was usually a member of an ethnic minority who maintained strong ethnic ties, i.e., Jews, Gypsies.

In contrast to the typical characterization of the stranger, entertainers come to the field from several paths: some choose; some are chosen. Indeed, some are members of ethnic minorities that have an entertainment tradition, while others choose entertainment from economic necessity. However, once chosen most entertainers are by necessity nomads, traveling from community to community, not bound by the norms and rules of societies through which they pass. Consequently, they were perceived as deviant by their hosts and were free to engage in deviant behavior.

Both psychologists and sociologists have painted the entertainer with a deviant brush. They have characterized show people as exhibitionist, egocentric, narcissistic, and frequently addicted to alcohol, illicit drugs and sex (Fisher & Fisher 1981; Fenichel 1946; Lane 1960 for example). Though anthropologists and sociologists are less likely than psychologists to examine the personality characteristics of performers, they frequently describe the working conditions which foster deviant behavior. Research on Gypsies (Sway 1988), strippers (Boles 1974; Ronai & Ellis 1989; Skipper & McCaghy 1971), carnies (Easto &Truzzi 1974) and comics

(Salutin 1973; Mintz 1985), female impersonators (Tewksbury 1993) point to the problems associated with a life in show business. Separation from family, easy access to alcohol and drugs, stigmatization, loneliness, and constant travel are just a few of the work problems identified. Moreover, entertainers, unless they are stars, are powerless relative to owners/managers. As there are always more performers than jobs, the processes of obtaining and keeping jobs are time consuming, debilitating and anything but ego enhancing. Essentially, the performer is hired and fired at the whim of the boss.

Research in the deviance tradition sees the entertainer as a person apart, a person who is estranged from traditional ties of family, community, and even nation. While the performer may be reviled, harassed and discriminated against, she is relatively free of societal strictures. She has the freedom to violate social norms. There are advantages to the role of stranger.

Entertainer as culture worker. A developing body of research focuses on the culture industry and its workers (Menger 1999; Friedman 1990; Bielby & Bielby 1999). Menger (1999) states that there are three competing hypotheses explaining why culture workers stay in that field in spite of the high rates of unemployment, underemployment and low wages. Love of the art is one explanation, but it is, as he points out, a tautological argument. Secondly, culture workers may be risk seekers who operate with a "probabilistic miscalculation" much like lottery players who believe that their numbers must eventually come up. Finally, he cites the economic theory of "equalizing differences", meaning that the psychic rewards compensate for the many drawbacks associated with work in the culture industry.

The focus of this research is on entertainers as culture workers. Using the sample of biographies, I examine the processes involved in occupational choice, socialization and career patterns. Studies of culture industry workers include art photographers (Giuffre 1999), dance musicians (MacLeod 1993), actors (Friedman 1990) and screen writers (Bielby & Bielby 1999) as well as the general structure of the culture industry (Caves 2000). This important, though limited, body of research illuminates the key characteristics of work in the culture industry from which a number of contingencies flow.

There are more applicants than jobs. Those who hire have significant power over those seeking jobs. Job hunting is an important component of worker experiences. Culture workers must be able and willing to perform many jobs while maintaining their culture worker identity, e.g., musician, actor, mime.

Reputation is the key ingredient in defining success in the culture industry or "you're only as good as your last picture." In contrast to many occupations in which human capital, i.e., education, training, seniority, are determiners of employability, one's current reputation is a key resource, and that resource atrophies rapidly over time (Bielby & Bielby 1999). All a culture worker has to sell is his/her reputation. If a concert promoter wants Bruce Springsteen, no one else will do. The promoter will have to pay whatever Springsteen demands. However, if Springsteen concerts fail to draw crowds, the money he can demand diminishes accordingly. Arguments like "I've played to packed houses" are of no avail. The history of show business is replete with examples of former stars who could not find work.

The quality of a culture worker's product is impossible to objectively evaluate. Culture workers who are successful are usually said to be more "talented" than their peers, but this is a tautological argument. By what standards do we judge the work product of Bob Hope against competing comics, or Norman Mailer against competing novelists? Hope may have had better writers and Mailer better editors. Some find Hope funny; others do not. The reward system in the culture industry may or may not be tied to any objective standard of excellence. Success in the marketplace is almost the sole criterion by which culture workers, particularly those in popular culture, are judged. Norman Mailer may or may not be a "better" writer than Stephen King, but he is certainly not as financially successful. Finally,

Cultural workers' products are often highly individualistic. Each culture worker seeks to create a product(s) which reflects his/her vision, style, talent and capabilities. Culture workers view themselves as having a special *gift* which it is their duty to communicate. Painters, novelists, and even pop singers may possess *the gift*. For the entertainer fundamental to this process of developing and communicating *the gift* is the creation of a persona and an act. Once created, the entertainer seeks, often with the help of agents and managers, to market that persona/act package. If the package is in demand, the entertainer gets work. All the entertainer has to sell is the package.

These two theoretical streams, deviance and culture work, are not antithetical, and it is my argument that they are closely joined in explaining the entertainer. The structure of culture work, particularly in the live entertainment industry, facilitates deviant behavior. I also argue that a personality characteristic of entertainers predisposes them to certain behaviors currently deemed deviant. The chapters in this book illuminate the processes by which some individuals, usually at a very young age, choose a career path which delivers great psychic rewards, but, often, at great cost.

This book is organized into twelve chapters. Chapters One and Two present a history of entertainers, beginning with the first entertainer/specialists, the shamans, to the present. Two findings are key: the persistence of the five categories of entertainers and the complex of problems associated with culture work.

Chapter Three reviews social science literature on entertainment as an occupation and on the personality characteristics of performers. Chapter Four describes the processes of sample selection and coding used in the study. Data on the demographic and family background characteristics of the sample are included .Chapter Five describes the process of occupational choice, illustrating how and when entertainers make their start in show business. The key players in facilitating that choice are identified, and their contributions detailed. Chapter Six focuses on the three primary entry-level career tracks while Chapter Seven provides a description of the early occupational socialization of these performers: how they developed an act and a persona.
The career tracks of entertainers, as related to the venues in which they primarily perform, is the heart of Chapter Eight. The contingencies associated

with playing clubs, outdoor venues, e.g., the circus, the carnival, and stages are discussed.

Because most entertainers are still "strangers" who must constantly travel, their choice of occupation affects their relationships with others, especially spouses, lovers and children. Chapter Nine focuses on the personal lives of the men and women in the sample while Chapter Ten describes the satisfactions and dissatisfactions of those show people. In Chapter Eleven I try to answer the question: "why do they persist?" Borrowing from motivational psychology, I use the "need for power" (n Power) concept as an explanation of why many performers stay in the field in spite of its drawbacks, and I show how some exhibit the Expansive Profligate Impulse(EPI) which is associated with those who have a high need for power.

Chapter Twelve concludes this research by briefly reviewing the findings in relation to the work contingencies associated with the culture industry. For live performers the psychic rewards associated with sharing *the gift* with the audience is incomparable. Only through live performance can the entertainer attain the psychic high. The entertainer works for and embraces the love/adulation/worship which the audience delivers when he/she has communicated *the gift*.

When my husband and I (Rex Dane and assistant) started in show business over fifty years ago, Don (my husband) believed he had the *gift*. Mind reading is an especially high risk act; the performer either amazes the audience or falls flat on his face. Stories about mind readers, mentalists, and other magic performers whose acts spectacularly fail are legend. These practitioners who perform high risk acts stare catastrophe in the face each time they stand on the stage. Eventually, Rex Dane decided to turn his *gift* to writing, and he wrote and published a number of books that are classics in the field of outdoor show business. Over the years, however, he continued to perform as a magician, monologist, violinist, and, occasionally, actor. No matter how much recognition he received from his readers, his first and continued romance was with live performance. After a particularly successful show, he would, like those in this sample, savor the reactions of his audience for weeks. "Did you see their faces?" "My finish blew them out of the water." "I could 'a gone for another half an hour."

The show folk whose life stories provide the data for this study detail the sacrifices that they made for *their art*. I'm sure that they, like others in the culture industry, would agree that it was worth it.

CHAPTER ONE

LET'S PUT ON A SHOW: THE HISTORY OF SHOW BUSINESS FROM THE BEGINNING UP TO THE 19TH CENTURY

In all societies there are individuals who specialize in providing entertainment: shamans, priests, storytellers, singers, musicians and mimes, as well as exotic dancers, stand-up comics and magicians. For some providing entertainment is ancillary to their primary occupation, while, for others, entertainment is their sole and full time function. Historians, anthropologists and other academicians, including those who study performance (Bauman 1984) have documented the history and development of a variety of entertainment forms and genres, e.g., vaudeville, jazz, cabaret, the circus. Most of this research, however, neglects to present a systematic study of the performers. While a number of biographies of important entertainers exist, the working lives and social positions of the thousands of itinerant musicians, music hall comics and circus acrobats have gone undocumented.

In this and the following chapter I present a brief history of entertainers with a view toward explicating the social positions and working conditions of these culture workers. As a general organizing principle I use the ideas developed by the musicologist, Alan Merriam (1964:140):

> The pattern of low status and high importance, deviant behavior and the capitalization of it cannot be said to characterize musicians in all societies, but it seems to be a basic organization for a number of groups in a rather remarkable world distribution.

Reports on entertainers in pre-literate societies are usually idiosyncratic, incomplete and often biased. Still using the available data, and Merriam's insights, I have attempted to knit together disparate accounts into a somewhat coherent picture of an ever-evolving occupation.

Entertainers in Tribal Societies. The origins of the first entertainers are lost to us, but probably they were individuals who specialized in music, storytelling and drama. Cave paintings which portray huntsmen blowing antler "horns" suggest that some early hunters also made music (Harwood 1984).

Humans are storytellers (*homo narrans*) as narration may be the earliest form of human communication (Fisher 1984). Drama developed from storytelling as tale tellers began to act out their stories. Most of the early dramatists were shamans who, while in a trance, enacted their cultures' myths. Lommel (1967) argued that the shaman was the first "artistically active man" who was singer, dancer, painter, magician, and theatrical producer. Shamans were central to the community life of the hunting tribes; they interpreted the myths, approached the deities, and healed the relationship between the community and its gods. All forms of variety entertainment found today originated with shamans, including ventriloquism, sword swallowing, close-up magic, rope tricks, puppetry, fire walking, acrobatics and escapes. The shaman/ventriloquist enabled the deity to "speak" and sleight-of-hand manipulations brought forth demons out of the mouths of the "possessed." Kirby (1975) argued that the dance/drama rituals found in many religious and secular performances, e.g., the Noh Theater in Japan, are descendants of the shaman-created ritual enactments.

Though shamans were important to the well-being of their communities, they were considered aberrant and dangerous as they held the power to bring the wrath of the deities on enemies or withhold cures from the sick. Shamans, and later priests, were set apart from others in the community because of their awesome powers. Thus, from the very beginning, entertainment was associated with power, danger, and mystery.

Communal activities in tribal societies involved singing, dancing and storytelling with most villagers participating. However, some individuals specialize in providing amusements. Those who are not full time entertainers are rewarded with gifts; for example, the Australian aborigine tribes use songmen and dancers who, in exchange for gifts, lead festivals and other community activities (Berndt & Berndt 1964), while the Shona mbira players are usually paid for their performances (Berliner 1978).

The presence of entertainers is often essential to weddings, festivals, religious services, and various celebratory activities. Mbira players are essential to the correct enactment of religious observances during the *bira*, a key religious event (Berliner 1978). Among the Tumbuka the dancer/healer is the central performer in the sacred healing dance (Friedson 1996).

Many of the reports about performers in tribal societies document their reputation for deviant behavior. In his ethnography of the Trobriand Islanders Malinowski (1925) reported that a well known singer was said to be engaging in sexual relations with his sister, a violation of the incest taboo, punishable by death. However, the villagers excused his behavior saying, in effect, "You know how musicians are."

Most entertainers are male and, generally, have reputations as promiscuous, drunken, lazy, and otherwise unstable. Merriam (1964) reported that the Basongye informants characterized musicians as "lazy, heavy drinking, impotent, physically weak and poor marriage risks." Ames (1973) interviewed 201 Hausa individuals who labeled musicians as "lazy, sly, dishonest, adulterous and servile." Musicians are also labeled as homosexual, bisexual or physically handicapped (Merriam 1964; Blacking 1995; Barish 1985). In sum, full time entertainers are often described similarly to this description of musicians:

> Only thieves, men who deal with feces in their work, praise shouters, strong-men, magicians, female impersonators, professional gamblers, kashewa dancers, and pimps are rated as low as or lower than musicians (Ames 1973:156).

Female entertainers are often labeled as promiscuous and licentious (Ames 1973; Koskoff 1987) as they frequently perform in "immoral" venues such as bars and are perceived as being out from under the control of male kin.

Entertainers in the Agricultural Civilizations and Europe to the 19th Century. The domestication of grains made large scale agriculture possible, and, thus, gave rise to the early civilizations: Egypt, Mesopotamia, India and China, beginning around 5,000 BCE. The birth of civilization changed human social organization dramatically, giving rise to both large cities and an increase in differences in wealth and power between the warrior/land-owning class and almost everybody else. These civilizations developed highly stratified, rigid social systems in which individuals were placed in a hierarchy of prestige and power.

Gerhard Lenski (1966) identified several classes/castes found in agricultural societies: 1) rulers and their retainers, e.g., administrators, soldiers, etc.; 2) priests; 3) merchants and artisans; 4) peasants, serfs and some slaves (slaves were variously positioned; some were administrators, personal retainers or artisans); and 5) unclean or degraded classes and expendables, e.g., prostitutes, beggars, coolies, gamblers and entertainers. The rights, privileges, and obligations of members of each of these classes/castes were spelled out in minute detail (Lenski 1966; Dumont 1970). The amount of mobility varied between societies. Both caste (no mobility), class (some mobility) and slave systems often operated simultaneously within the same society. Also, with the development of large scale agriculture the division of labor increased as there was sufficient surplus wealth so that artisans, merchants, laborers and entertainers could flourish. Sumptuous banquets, magnificent palaces, ornate clothing and adornments testified to the wealth and power of the nobility. The rulers also vied with each other to present elaborate entertainments for their guests as well as occasional festivals for the general public. Full time performers became important, indeed necessary, to the operation of the courts.

Most courts had fools attached to them. Historical records attest to the presence of fools in the courts of Egypt, India, Greece, Rome and medieval Europe. Many fools were physically or mentally impaired and were often thought to have psychic powers. They provided entertainment to the court; some have likened the role of the fool to that of the contemporary political comic who "pokes fun" at those in power. "The fool has his niche in a divinely planned order of society, to whose dependent, ephemeral and often corrupt character it was his function to bear witness (Welsford 1935:285)."

Additionally, the merchants, artisans and some of the common laborers had enough free time and disposable income to enjoy professional performers who were hired to entertain at weddings and other special occasions. Generally at the bottom of the entertainer hierarchy were the street performers who *busked* on street corners, depending on a few coins from passersby.

Life in the Indus valley three thousand years ago as now is primarily organized around villages. Throughout most of its history and even today the caste system dominates Indian social organization, particularly the villages. There are six major castes, innumerable sub-castes and an outcaste, the Untouchables. Occupations are designated by caste position, and the Untouchables have the least desirable occupations. Most professional entertainers belong to low-status subcastes; for example, only the Sudra, a low caste, and outcastes may play wind instruments as the act of blowing on the instrument makes a high caste individual impure, and therefore, defiled (Dubois 1928). Over the centuries hundreds of thousands of traveling magicians, puppeteers, jugglers, snake charmers, and acrobats have performed in the cities and villages of India (Betelille 1965; Dube 1955).

An Englishman, L. H. Branson, published a little book entitled **Indian Conjuring** (no publishing date listed) about the magic tricks of three Indian *Jadoo-wallahs* or itinerant magicians. The author's primary informant, Shah Mohammed, was the son and grandson of *Jadoo-wallahs*, and traveled across India performing magic tricks, and, occasionally, singing. The career of Shah Mohammed illustrates the precariousness of the existence of street entertainers in India and elsewhere.

Women from all castes became temple dancers /prostitutes in permanent residence at major Hindu temples (Bowers 1953; Dubois 1928). These women (*devadasis*) were trained in Kathak, a classical Indian dance and were paid by the temple to dance and sexually serve temple devotees. Additionally, secular courtesan/performers (*nautch girls*) were attached to the courts (Post 1987).

In addition to solo performers like Shah Mohammed over the centuries many entertainment troupes have roamed over the country. These troupes usually consist of a number of interrelated men and women who perform "revues" which might include singing, dancing, dramatic storytelling and magic. The female members may also engage in prostitution. The most well-known of these bands are the Gypsies who have, over the centuries, traveled all over the world.

The Gypsies or Rom probably left India around 1,000 years ago, first traveling to Persia where they were made slaves. From Persia some of the Rom moved into Turkey and then to Russia and Eastern Europe; from there they migrated to the rest of Europe and eventually to the United States. After leaving Persia some Rom headed to North Africa and from there to Spain.

The Rom are nomads and have, over the centuries, become adept at adapting to the local environment. They find and exploit niches such as repairing pots and pans, driveways and septic tanks, trading horses and selling used clothing. In Mexico they specialize in providing outdoor movies (cine *ambulante*) to poor villagers. However, they have always had a reputation as entertainers and fortunetellers (Sutherland 1975; Sway 1984).

Singing, dancing and playing musical instruments have traditionally been part of the Rom's repertoire. Also, they often use performing animals like horses and bears as well as magic tricks. They are adept at a number of sleight-of-hand tricks which are useful in performance as well as in fortunetelling. The Rom incorporate standard variety acts, e.g., juggling, puppetry, acrobatics, sword swallowing, in their street performances In Spain Gypsies, called *Gitanos* are major contributors to flamenco, the national dance. In Eastern Europe Rom music has strongly influenced both folk and commercial dance music. While they have used instruments available in the countries where they travel, they are most closely associated with the violin, the guitar and the cymbalom.

As well as entertaining the Rom have a reputation for fortunetelling. As they passed through the various countries in their travels they have foretold the future to rulers and commoners. They were often believed to have magic powers, to be able to cast the evil eye and cast out evil spirits. Currently, in the United States many Rom women maintain an *ofisa* where they tell fortunes, find lost or missing people and money and take off curses (Boles 1968). One of the standard tricks that Rom women use to convince their clients that their money is cursed is to pull a "devil" out of an egg the client has brought from home. A trick similar to this was used by a number of Native American shamans for much the same purpose (Kirby 1975). During much of Chinese history castes, classes and slavery operated simultaneously. China produced a large number of performers including jugglers, dancing girls/prostitutes, actors, sword swallowers, riddle makers, imitators of village talk, imitators of street cries, acrobats and musicians (Gernet 1962; Yang 1956). Indeed, Gernet (1962) found a text written in 1280CE which listed 55 different types of entertainers; puppeteers were especially popular and some used real people with thin legs rather than wooden figures. The rulers established public amusement parks staffed by entertainers and dancing girls/prostitutes who also worked in bars and taverns as did transvestite dancer/prostitutes (Gernet 1962).

Typically, entertainers, like other "degraded and expendable" groups were relegated to the lower castes. For example, during the T'ang dynasty musicians were classified with descendants of convicts and forbidden to marry outside their caste (Yang 1956).

The Egyptian and Mesopotamian civilizations also were noted for their entertainers. The first recorded magic performance presented as entertainment occurred in Egypt around 1700BCE when Dedi, the conjuror, performed two illusions before the Pharaoh, Cheops (Burger & Neale 1995). Dedi cut off the head of a goose and then restored it, a popular illusion to this day.

The word *magic* itself comes from the Greek and refers to a priestly clan (*magoi*) who migrated to Greece from ancient Iran (Luck, 1986; Burger & Neale 1995). The *magoi* were believed to have many magic powers and were greatly feared.

The Middle Eastern and Egyptian courts supported many entertainers; further, the large cities in these empires, e.g., Memphis, Baghdad, Thebes teemed with street entertainers, as they do today. Street performers still travel through Egypt and the Middle East performing magic tricks, singing and dancing. Dramatic storytelling is a popular entertainment as many villagers are illiterate and learn the history of the culture and religion from these vagabond storytellers.

Occupational specialization increased dramatically in Japan between the 9th and 10th centuries CE (Price 1968), and, like China and India, Japanese society was organized into castes, classes and slaves. The *hinin* or not-people were a subcaste of the outcastes and included puppeteers and monkey show performers as well as prostitutes and beggars. It was generally agreed that "actors were a social group lower than merchants and only a little above the pariah caste (Shively 1968:262)."

As in many other countries Japanese female performers were associated with both religion and dance. Kabuki originated as a dance performed at shrines by females associated with the temples; however, in the 1600s these temple dancers began touring the provinces while engaging in prostitution after their performances (Shively 1968; Ashihara 1965). The shogun replaced the female dancers with young boys which led to an increase in male prostitution; eventually, until the end of WWII, adult males performed all the adult roles in Kabuki. In 2003 an all male Kabuki troupe performed in Kyoto.

In many societies female performers are assumed to be prostitutes. In Tunisia the first female performers were slaves; so well into the 20th Century females who performed publically were called "Christian slave girls."

> The public professional female musician . . . has descended directly from the pleasure palaces of the golden past, from the slave harem, from the libidinous dream world of the Thousand and One Nights, or from the more sordid public tavern (Jones 1987:79-80).

Among the Javanese the female singer/dancers were also associated with prostitution:

> The word *taledhek* (singer/dancer) has the same root as *ngeledhek* which means "to tempt" (Sutton 1987:112)." Also in Northern India the Kanjar women are noted as dancers and prostitutes (Berland 1982).

Greeks and Romans held ambivalent attitudes toward entertainment and entertainers. Even though Greeks produced some of the world's greatest theater, public performers were generally relegated to the lower ranks (Barish 1981). Plato banned theater from his Republic. In Rome prejudice against the theater peaked during the early days of the empire. Actors were denied civil rights, could not engage in military service, could be beaten at will by the police, could not leave their occupation for another, and were forced to coerce their children into becoming actors.

> Like prostitution the stage had become to be thought of as a necessary evil. As it was evil, its practitioners had to be humiliated and punished for their part in it. But as it was necessary, they had to be prevented from making their escape from it, since its continuance needs to be guaranteed. (Barish1981:42).

The early Christian church also took a dim view of theatrics and performers. In order to receive the sacraments actors had to renounce their profession, an act forbidden by the state (Barish 1981). Gradually, the church modified its view of the theater and theatrical productions came under the control of the church and were used to promulgate the faith. The ancient connection between religion and entertainment was re-established.

During the Middle Ages in Europe entertainers thrived. Troupes of traveling show folks performed at the castles as well as in the villages, not only amusing their audiences but also bringing news and gossip. Some dramas developed out of and were elaborations of the Christian Mass, while folk mummers' plays seem to have a secular origin (Kirby 1978). In England between 1300 and 1600 CE entertainment was dominated by the great cycle plays, particularly the Corpus Christi dramas (Hanks 1986).

Over the ensuing centuries an increasingly great gulf separated popular entertainment from the church so that by the 15th Century both the Catholic and Protestant churches condemned much of the popular theater (Harwood 1984). With the rise of Puritanism during the 17th century condemnation of public entertainment increased. In 1633 Prynne published **Histriomastix**, an encyclopedia of antitheatrical lore which pilloried public performers (Barish 1981).

While the wealthy actively pursued leisure and recreation, the "lower classes" were strongly discouraged from enjoying what little free time they had in leisurely pursuits (Malcolmson 1973). Idleness was regarded as the "fruitful root of every vice."

> In Works of Labour or of Skill
> I would be busy too:
> For Satan finds some Mischief still
> For idle Hands to do (Watts 1926).

In Russia the *skomorokhi* or minstrels were originally pagan priests who used horns, string instruments and trained bears as part of their performing and divining activities (Zguta 1978). They performed at weddings, held religious services, foretold the future and presided over community festivities; however, as they were accused of Satanism by Greek Orthodox clergy, they gradually abandoned their religious activities and became full time minstrels. Most were part of the *tsiaglye liudi* or common class and were very poor and had reputations as thieves and prostitutes.

> One cannot help but wonder whether these thefts were motivated by malice and greed or were simply the acts of desperate men trying to keep body and soul together. After all these were among the poorest members of society, and they could rarely eke out an existence on their meager professional earnings (Zguta 1978:48).

In Germany during the Middle Ages the social position of musicians was determined by two key factors: the type of instrument they played, and the organization with which they were affiliated. Trumpet players had high prestige (relative to other musicians) because trumpets provided the fanfares for the nobility (Salem 1983). Those who traveled from court to court (like Mozart) had the most prestige; those attached to a court were second, and those employed by municipalities (town musicians) third (Petzoldt 1983). Itinerant folk musicians (*spielmann*) were accorded the least prestige and often were deemed outside the class system (Salem 1983).

Though medieval musicians were often treated as pariahs, they were important; German weddings were not legal unless musicians were present (Salem 1983). However important they were to the functioning of the courts and communities which employed them, they were considered deviant and dangerous. Itinerant musicians were believed to have magic and divinatory powers i.e., The Pied Piper of Hamlin, and were frequently accused of witchcraft (Krickeberg 1983). Most musicians were not allowed to swear an oath, hold property, receive legal damages for harms, or pass property to their children (Salem 1983; Krickeberg 1983). Some itinerant musical troupes included female performers who were usually labeled as prostitutes (*concubinen ofte spilfrowen);* these women sometimes played the barrel organ and danced (Krickeberg 1983).

In England actors and other show folks were generally accorded low status. In 1572 parliament passed an act regulating the "Punishment of Vagabonds and the Relief of the Poor and Impotent." Under its provisions show people were classed as rogues and vagabonds unless they were in the paid service of a "Baron of the Realm" or any other personage of greater degree (Harwood 1984). For the first offense the actor was whipped and branded; for the third he was executed. Through the 17th Century the Catholic Church in France excommunicated show people (Harwood 1984). Entertainers were equated with whores and whoremasters and were forbidden to receive the sacraments and denied Christian burial.

Currently, in all parts of the globe entertainers, particularly itinerant street performers are fulfilling their age-old functions: spreading the news, helping people celebrate festive occasions and contributing to a more positive quality of life (Kasule 1998; Aptekar 1991).

As the dawn of the Industrial revolution approached, entertainers' connections to organized religion were severed, and they embraced secular society, the city, and their central role in developing and spreading popular culture.

This review of the early history of entertainment and entertainers suggests that:

a) Entertainment has been closely associated with religion. Shamans and priests developed the first variety skills and used them to both entertain and mystify their audiences. Also women were often associated with religious institutions. They were often attached to temples as dancers/ singers/prostitutes.

b) Entertainers were frequently believed to have magic powers; they could foretell the future, restore missing objects, cure the sick and intercede with the deities. Because they were believed to have magic powers they were often feared.

c) Even though professional show people were important to the life of their communities they were accorded low status and were almost inevitably poor. They were often outside the caste/class systems of host societies and were, therefore, not governed by the rules that applied to others.

d) They were believed to engage in a range of deviant acts, i.e., stealing, kidnapping and murder, prostitution, drug and alcohol use, and all manner of sexual behaviors outside of the range of normative behavior.

e) They were "strangers" to most of their audiences; they came into the town or village, put on their show and left. Rumors of their powers and their misbehaviors preceded them into town and followed them when they left. Jewelry and sometimes children disappeared, wives were compromised, husbands had a secret adventure, and then life returned to normal until the next time "the show came to town."

Chapter Two

LET'S PUT ON A SHOW: THE HISTORY OF SHOW BUSINESS FROM THE 19TH CENTURY TO THE PRESENT

In the 16th and 17th centuries English country fairs were a major source of entertainment for rural people. Small circuses toured villages and larger towns (Truzzi 1968). However, increasingly, show folks gravitated to the city where there were eager audiences for their performances. The beginnings of the 19th century saw the development of leisure activities for all social classes. The growth of cities, changes in the labor process, and the increased numbers of middle class merchants, artisans and professionals allowed for the expansion of the all types of culture workers including entertainers.

In the city there were entertainments for all; for the rich private theaters featuring risqué plays enthralled the adventurous; the middle classes favored popular revues and plays while the poor enjoyed street performers who worked for tips, i.e., *busking*. In his groundbreaking study (circa 1840s) of the poor Henry Mayhew (1968) interviewed street performers including Punch and Judy players, ratcatchers, fire eaters, snake swallowers, strolling actors (*mummers*), street reciters, silly billies, bagpipe players and exhibitors of trained dogs.

Most of those show people came from working class families, and many had run away from home or were orphans. Some were from show business families and learned their acts from kin; many were physically handicapped. One man who ran a peep show was crippled and had been orphaned and out on the street since age ten. "Old Blind Sarah" played the hurdy-gurdy; her father was a hatter and her mother a flower-maker. Sarah learned to play in a workhouse.

Many of those Mayhew interviewed felt that they had "come down in the world"; a Punch and Judy performer had been a footman and an acrobat on the stage but now was forced to work on the street. Some were alcoholics and/ or thieves while others worked hard to support their families. All in all street performing was a low status, low pay job.

During the 19th century in both Europe and the United States entertainment forms continued to evolve. While circuses and street performance continued to flourish, the expanding middle class gravitated to the legitimate theater. Acting was still generally considered a marginal occupation, not to be considered by respectable men and women.

> Victorian performers were an unusual socioeconomic group. Unlike other professionals, they were recruited from all classes of society. While performers repeatedly demonstrated that class origins could be defied by hard work, talent or strategic marital alliances to secure place in the most select company, others lived with the most impoverished classes. Unlike other occupational groups performers' incomes spanned the highest upper middle class salary and the lower working class wage, and were earned in work places that ranged in status from patent theaters to penny saloons (Davis 1991:3).

The gradual rise in status of actors was largely due to increased recruitment of men and women from middle class families into the theater. Sanderson (1984) reviewed the family backgrounds of some prominent actors and actresses and found that the majority of actresses had either professional or theatrical family histories while most actors came from professional families. Further, McArthur (1984) examined census data for the United States in 1900 and found that a large percentage of actors' fathers were professionals or managers.

The middle of the 19th century saw the beginnings of the star system; actors and actresses were gaining notoriety beyond the stage, and audiences became interested in their lives outside the theater. David Garrick, the first superstar of the London Theater, did not tell his family of his profession until his success in **Richard III** (Harwood 1984). Others followed: Henry Irving, Ellen Terry, Sarah Bernhardt, and Edwin Booth in the United States.

Actors and actresses in the legitimate theater were caught in a dilemma:

they acknowledged the marginality of their status as professionals by both wanting to maintain their separateness as actors while seeking middle class respectability. "Professionalization became a driving impulse within the acting world in the last decade of the 19th century as actors looked outward for models of social advancement (McArthur 1984:83-4)."

Conversely, actors wanted to be identified as "in the theater" and to this end they dressed, talked, and behaved differently from those "not in the business." The stereotypical actor of the time dressed flamboyantly, talked loudly about his show business experiences and often used alcohol or other drugs to excess. Actresses dressed ostentatiously in frocks which enhanced their physical attributes. Many pretended to be more sexually experienced than they, in fact, were.

While actors and actresses in the legitimate theater wrestled with their status dilemma, new forms of entertainment emerged which appealed not only to the middle class but also to the working class who had money and free time. With the gradual improvement of roads in the mid 19th century an increasing number of show folks took to the open road. Circuses and carnivals played small towns; at their peak in 1903 1100 circuses toured in the United States (Truzzi 1968). Other types include: repertoire tent shows presenting stock plays like **The Drunkard and Uncle Tom's Cabin** as well as medicine shows which provided live theater as well as miracle cures. Wild West extravaganzas, showboats, and traveling exhibits added to the mix.

For show people there was a general route of professional upward mobility. Street entertaining marked the beginnings of a career (and sometimes the end). Touring with a troupe followed: circuses, carnivals, Wild West shows, and medicine shows. Circuses had more prestige than carnivals, and both had more than medicine shows. Repertory Theater was more prestigious than carnivals and circuses. Finally, a performer might make the transition to a major company: vaudeville, burlesque, minstrels, Broadway. Until the advent of talking pictures Broadway stage productions were the benchmarks of show business success.

> The 1906-07 season would prove to be the most active in the history of the American theatre, with hundreds of professional touring shows, more than a thousand active vaudeville theatres, minstrelsy, burlesque, stock companies, and a dozen circuses. More than thirty thousand people made their living as performers (Goldman 1991:23).

Many of the stars of the 20th century who are included in sample of entertainers used in this book got their start in these new entertainment forms, e.g., Al Jolson, Fanny Brice, Jack Benny, Will Rogers, Jackie Gleason, Burns and Allen, Red Skelton. Some of these stars made the transition from vaudeville to film and radio to television. In order to understand the work environments in which these culture workers labored, I provide a brief history of various key entertainment forms which developed in the late 19th and early 20th centuries.

Vaudeville. In London the first music hall opened in 1852 and by 1920, 69 venues for variety acts operated in the London area (Wilmut 1960). The music hall and vaudeville developed out of saloon/bar culture. A typical music hall bill featured a star, usually a singer or comic, as well as a number of variety artists, e.g., jugglers, magicians, acrobats. Both performers and audience were from the working class, and the programs were considered bawdy by the middle class. The young women in the choruses were considered little better than prostitutes. The pay and living conditions of the performers were abominable; most barely earned enough to survive. They lived in boarding and rooming houses, frequently without heat. The life of a music hall performer is vividly portrayed by Lawrence Olivier in **The Entertainer.**

Music halls were exported to the United States in the form of vaudeville and appealed primarily to working class and immigrant audiences who found standard comic routines, ethnic humor and pathos familiar. Vaudeville flourished between 1890 and the 1920s, and many of the early movie stars in both England and the United States got their start playing variety, e.g., Cary Grant, Charlie Chaplin, Stan Laurel, The Marx Brothers, Buster Keaton and Bob Hope.

Vaudeville was organized into circuits, and performers were hired to tour a given circuit. The two major circuits were the Keith and the Orpheum, and the two small-time were the Pantages and Loews. Beyond these four there were smaller circuits, including one using all Black acts, as well as a number of independent theaters.

The backbone of vaudeville was low comedy: dialect humor, eccentric dancing, pratfalls, exaggerated costumes and facial makeup. Acrobats, singers, and magicians rounded out the bill, but the heart of vaudeville was comedy in dialect. Most of the major vaudeville stars were comedy teams like Smith and Dale and Weber and Fields.

Performers with Keith only did two shows a day and played the same theater for a week. The dressing rooms were usually heated, and the salary afforded a living, if not luxury. Those playing the small-time did from three to six shows daily and made considerably less money. Salaries for vaudeville headliners generally averaged between $150 and $3,000 a week, depending on the circuit with which the performer was affiliated (Goldman 1991). The social status of small-time show folks was low, and they were often taunted and ridiculed by the locals, particularly if their act was not well received. Harpo Marx (1961:103-4) recalled his early days in vaudeville:

> Looking back, I simply don't know how we survived it. Those early days on the road were pure unmitigated hell. They made my early days on the streets of the East Side seem like a long recess. If the audiences didn't like us we had no trouble finding it out. We were pelted with sticks, bricks, spitballs, cigar butts, peach pits, and chewed out stalks of sugar cane.

However, other performers like Fanny Brice recalled their experiences in vaudeville with great fondness, while acknowledging the importance of vaudeville and burlesque in training performers:

> The performer is different today . . . Years ago we had a school. The school was vaudeville and burlesque. You knocked around. So it seasoned you. Made a mensch of you. So it gave you an interesting background before you clicked (Goldman 1991:5).

The Keith and Orpheum circuits slowly but inexorably dominated vaudeville, driving out the competition. In their efforts to broaden their appeal to the middle class, vaudeville impresarios added more "highbrow" acts, e.g., opera singers, Shakespearean actors. Celebrities including Helen Keller told their life stories from the stage. As a result, vaudeville became homogenized, sanitized, boring and predictable. And, of course, competition in the forms of radio and moving pictures attracted an ever-increasing number of customers. Gradually, vaudeville died, and talking pictures ascended. But, of course, no viable entertainment form disappears entirely. Many of the early television shows like Milton Berle's and Bob Hope's were vaudeville on tape. Ed Sullivan's **Toast of the Town** was strictly vaudeville. A few seasons ago Broadway imported a very popular British play modeled on the English music hall, **The Play What I Wrote.**

Vaudeville performers, like their circus and carnival peers, were often related; there were brother and sister acts, husband and wife teams, and sometimes entire families like the Foys or the Marx Brothers. Consequently, many performers were the children of performers and learned their craft by appearing on stage as children. Of course, many vaudevillians came from working or middle class families and had no previous show business experience. Vaudevillians learned on the job through trial and error, begging, borrowing and stealing dance steps, jokes, and bits of business from other performers. Though most vaudevillians were White, a substantial number of Blacks performed in the major circuits, particularly after the strike led by the actors' union, The White Rats. When members of the White Rats (rats is star spelled backwards) struck, management hired Black performers who, thus, got a foothold in the better paying circuits.

Minstrel Shows. America developed a unique entertainment form: the minstrel show which flowered between the 1840s and the 1870s (Bean, Hatch & McNamara 1996; Mahar 1998; Toll 1977). America's first native-born professional actor, John Durang, worked in blackface, and through the years large numbers of both White and Black performers wore burnt cork.

The minstrel show consisted of several segments including the *olio* which featured musical numbers, comedy and skits. Stephen Foster wrote songs like **De Camptown Races** for minstrels. As there were no female performers, men impersonated women. Two primary impresarios were Lew Dockstader and George Christy. A central focus of the minstrel show was the dialogue between the interlocutor who represented middle class values and the other performers who played either rural rubes or citified dandies.

A number of major stars came out of the minstrel and blackface experience. T. D. Rice created Jim Crow and his famous dance:

Weel about and turn about
And do jis so,
Eb'ry time I weel about
And jump Jim Crow, (published by E. Riley in early 1830s)

Together with Rice, Lew Dockstader, George Christy, Patrick Francis and Dan Emmett were among the early minstrel stars. William Henry Lane, aka Master Juba, is credited with the invention of the tap dance. Lane, who grew up in the infamous "Five Points" area of New York City, combined African dance steps with the Irish "jig" to create the tap dance (Hanners 1993). After the end of the Civil War, several all Black troupes, i.e., Georgia Slave Troupe Minstrels, Georgia Minstrels toured. While the staging and costumes of the major companies were very elaborate, the living conditions of the employees were similar to that endured by most vaudeville and burlesque performers.

Blackface was not relegated just to the minstrel show; singers, comics and dancers appearing in vaudeville or in stage plays often appeared in burnt cork. Minstrel shows became a route of upward mobility for many show folks. A number of show business "greats" including Al Jolson, Bert Williams, Bob Hope, Ma Rainey, Ornette Coleman, Oliver Hardy, Roy Acuff and Gene Autry performed in blackface during their careers. The great torch singer, Sophie Tucker, often closed her act by removing one glove so the audience could see she was White.

Gradually enthusiasm for the minstrel show and racial "humor" dimmed. "Coon songs" gradually disappeared from vaudeville and the Broadway stage (Lott 1993). In the United States in the 1950s there were occasional minstrel troupes playing in the South and West. Great Britain imported the minstrel show, and it continued in popularity there until the 1970s. For many the minstrel show is an embarrassment. However, like vaudeville, minstrelsy keeps reemerging. Lhamon (1996) discusses the commonalities between minstrel and blackface humor and contemporary television programs and urban music. The great Black comic, Redd Foxx, acknowledged the debt he owed to the old **Amos and Andy** radio programs for the material he used on his own television show. In the 1950s Eddie Cantor performed in blackface on **The Ed Sullivan Show** and in the 1990s the English television comic, Benny Hill, used White actors in blackface employing plantation dialects. Additionally, through the 1950s various cartoon characters were portrayed in blackface. Within the last decade a Broadway musical focused on minstrelsy but closed before its New York premier.

Very little is known about the backgrounds of most minstrel performers. As it was a new form and short-lived, it is probable that fewer minstrel show people were children of show people than was true of vaudevillians. The majority of the performers in the *olio*, i.e., the variety segment, attempted, like Al Jolson, to move into vaudeville or the Broadway stage. Some made it; others did not.

Burlesque. Going back to the temple dancers of India, Rome and Japan, show business has always been about sex. Presenting attractive females (and sometimes males) attired in outfits which augment their natural attractions has always been a crowd pleaser. Show men have used women to gather a crowd (*tip*) and entice the locals to part with their money. Costuming female performers so as to show them off to the best effect while conforming to "community standards" is both an art and a craft. Decisions about what part and how much of the flesh to bare are crucial to the success of much theatrical fare.

The great fan dancer, Sally Rand, defined showgirl as "a young woman who is tall, over 5'8", beautiful, whose sole function is to look beautiful, walk beautifully, decorate a stage, and be a clothes horse (personal communication)." Rand distinguishes between the showgirl and the *pony* "who is a little girl who dances."

Showgirls and ponies are the foot soldiers of much of commercial theater: variety, vaudeville, burlesque, Broadway musicals, Las Vegas revues, strip clubs and the like. Showgirls trace their history from the temple dancer/ prostitute to the contemporary Broadway chorus girl. In Fin de Siecle France the showgirl was acknowledged as a combination of prostitute and entertainer (Stuart 1996). The famous showgirls of that period include Josephine Baker, Mata Hari, Colette, Barbette (who was actually a female impersonator), Gaby Deslys and Adah Isaacs Menken. The heyday of the showgirl occurred during the 1920s when Flo Ziegfield and Earl Carroll built their elaborate productions around them.

The everyday lives of showgirls were documented by Colette who was both a showgirl herself and a writer. Poverty, hunger, cold, and desperation were typical conditions in which they lived. They feared middle age when their usefulness would end. Some hoped to marry a well-to-do man before they got too old to appear on the stage. Stuart (1996:60) reproduces some of the "rules" for showgirls published anonymously in Britain in 1907:

> Never make any suggestion or say 'I think'. There will only be trouble if you do.
> Stout ladies are better than lean.
> The photographs of celebrities that you see around the room mean nothing, so don't be impressed into paying more because of them— they don't make the sheets dry, or the cooking good.
>
> Don't let your mother die more than twice during the run of the piece.

When you address a letter to a gentleman always put 'Esq.,' after his name, not 'Mr.', before it. Many a wife has learnt the truth through the omission, Mr. and Mrs. are so alike. It is worth drinking a lemon squash if there is any chance of his marrying you.

Don't stare too hard at the man when he pays the bill or bite any of the coins you may have suspicions about.

A few stars made very large salaries and became famous. A number of early movie and stage stars began their careers as showgirls including Marlene Dietrich, Mary Pickford, Mabel Norman, Mae West, Judy Holiday, Joan Crawford, Paulette Goddard and Barbara Stanwyck.

Prior to WWII many English variety productions featured nude performers. Women and men were permitted to stand on the stage nude as long as they neither moved nor spoke. Producers put together tableau of well-known historical or mythological scenes featuring naked performers striking dramatic poses. A major impresario of the time is quoted as saying (Wilmut 1960:215):"We had nudes in lions' cages, nudes in ice, and the only Chinese nudes in Europe." Revolving stages which allowed the performers to be viewed from all angles were popular. Since variety theaters were under the jurisdiction of the Lord Chamberlain, he had to approve the poses as well as the billing for the performances. He rejected one show, **This Is the Show,** because the promoter used only the first letter of each word in his billing (Wilmut 1960).

Productions featuring nude performers appeared in New York City as well. Gradually, however, tableau fell out of favor and was replaced by burlesque. The term burlesque is derived from the Italian *burlesco* meaning joke (Baddeley 1952). In the 17th century burlesque meant the debasement of classical writers, and in the following century it included the idea of the mock-heroic as in **The Rape of the Lock.** The essence of burlesque, as a style, is that it laughs at sacred things: love, motherhood, duty, nobility, etc.

Burlesque originated in Italy and spread to France and England. The first example of English burlesque was a skit by Chaucer dealing with chivalric romances. Many of England's most famous writers created burlesques: Fielding, Sheridan, Dickens and Gilbert. During the 19th century melodrama was introduced. Standard jokes, stock characters and situations increased:

"Jolly Jack Tar, the mother and child in the snow, the heroine who determined to suffer rather than follow the dictates of her heart, the idle rich, and the country bumpkin.

The beginning of American burlesque was the importation of an English production of **Hamlet** in 1828. This burlesque or travesty was very popular and led to a rash of travesties of the classics. The travesty was often the concluding segment of minstrel productions of which female impersonation was a frequent comic component. Eventually, however, the popularity of these burlesque travesties began to pale. A new dimension was added with the advent of Adah Isaacs Menken who, while wearing tights, was strapped to a horse in a play based on Bryon's poem **Mazeppa.** Theatrical producers immediately saw the future and it was wearing pink tights.

On September 12, 1866 at Niblo's Garden **The Black Crook** took New York by storm (Matlaw 1967).

The Black Crook is the acknowledged forerunner of modern burlesque because here, for the first time in the history of the American stage, female nudity was exhibited not as an integral part of the plot, but frankly and with bravado for its own crass and pleasant appeal (Zeidman 1967:23).

The cast included the principle dancer, Marie Bonfant, who was either 14 or 15 years old plus 80 female dancers (Matlaw 1967). The play made a net profit of $660,000 its first year and ran for 30 years. From then on burlesque changed direction----away from theater toward sex for its own sake. **The Black Crook** was followed by **Lydia Thompson and her Blondes** who opened at **Wood's Museum and Menagerie** on 34th Street in New York. Soon burlesque theaters abounded. During the 1890s burlesque productions assumed the form which typified them in their so-called "golden age." Pink tights, ethnic comedy, musical specialities and big production numbers filled out the bills. "Hootchy-kootchy" entered the American lexicon in the person of Little Egypt who was the hit of a world's fair. The *kootch* or belly dance migrated to carnival girls' shows; female performers were referred to as *kootch dancers.* Like vaudeville burlesque was organized into circuits called "wheels." By 1904 there were two wheels: the Columbia or Eastern and the Empire or Western. The wheels helped stabilize burlesque with a consequent improvement in the working conditions of the employees. At the same time the wheels routinized burlesque. A combination of worn-out routines and aging soubrettes resulted in vaudeville siphoning off most of the talent. From its apex in 1916 burlesque experienced a gradual decline.

The problems which beset burlesque were two-fold. Increasingly, politicians responded to citizens' concerns about "immorality" in burlesque by closing theaters. Competition from radio, moving pictures and other entertainment forms contributed to declining attendance. Perhaps, most importantly, burlesque failed to recruit young female performers:

> Fat, lean, scrawny, pockmarked, haggard and aged, fleshy thighs bulging from skin tights splashed with runway dirt, they lived on 'varicose alley', the runway on which they jiggled their breasts and compressed their buttocks (Zeidman 1967:110).

One production featured a "beef trust", a bevy of very over-weight performers in tights (Sally Rand, personal communication). In a word burlesque was dying; what saved it was stripping.

Ann Corio (1968) records what may have been the first strip in the United States. In 1908 Anna Held, the first wife of Flo Ziegfield was reported to have disrobed to a song titled "I'd Like to See a Little More of You." Around 1920 Mae Dix built an act around encouraging patrons to tear little strips of newspaper from her paper costume. However, Corio credits Hinda Wassau and Carrie Finnell the honor of being co-creators of the first strip-tease. Hinda Wassau, as the story goes, was scheduled to perform the shimmy, a vigorous dance involving shaking the body. Her costume got stuck before she got on stage. She went on stage and started her performance, and as she shimmied, her costume gradually fell to the floor. Ms. Wassau immediately recognized the potential of her innovation.

The story of Carrie Finnell is somewhat different. In 1928 she was performing at a theater in Cleveland, Ohio. As she wished to prolong her engagement, she hit on the idea of removing one item of her costume at each performance. She promised her audience she would remove one item of clothing each week for the limit of her engagement. She remained at the theater for 52 weeks (Corio 1968).

The work environment of the female performers in burlesque was difficult. The dressing rooms were often dirty and unheated. Except for the stars the pay was poor and the work hard. Some complained about the "degrading environment" in which customers shrouded themselves in heavy coats in order to conceal their "activities." Nevertheless, burlesque was home to a number of feature performers who became relatively famous and economically successful: Gypsy Rose Lee, Ann Corio, Rose La Rose, Margie Hart, Georgia Sothern, and Lily St. Cyr.

To become a successful feature stripper the performer had to develop a persona which included: the name on the marquee (Morgana the Wild One, Lady Sintana, The Swedish Blue Angel) the walk, costumes, makeup and hair styling, and, most importantly, the gimmick. The dancer might choose among a number of standard personas such as elegant and lady-like, or cute and bubbly, or, perhaps, mysterious sophisticate. The costumes, accessories and gimmick must reflect and enhance the persona. One performer used a trained bird to pluck off her costume, item by item. The great Carrie Finnell finished with an exhibition of tassel twirling which she evidently invented. Feature strippers "owned" their gimmicks, and woe to a new dancer who tried to steal a feature's gimmick.

Even though stripping was important to the survival of burlesque, comedy was always a major component of any burlesque show. There are a number of classic burlesque routines which comics memorized and performed over and over and over until some in the audience were as familiar with them as the comics. Gene Graham, who toured with his wife and two daughters and six-year-old son in a contemporary burlesque show titled **Best of Burlesk** used a burlesque routine he inherited from an old comic. His routine like the famous "Who's On First popularized by Abbott and Costello finds its humor in misunderstanding and confusion.

Burlesque produced a number of famous comics including Bert Lahr, Abbott and Costello, Phil Silvers, Red Skelton, Joe E. Brown, Eddie Cantor, Red Buttons, Jackie Gleason, Danny Thomas, Ed Wynn, and Bobby Clark. However successful they were, the comics were not paid as much as the feature strippers. In the 1930s Morton Minsky said that Phil Silvers was paid $250 a week while Minsky's top strippers made between $700 and $2000.

In the late 1930s and early 40s burlesque began to fade; the fabled **Minsky's** was closed as were a variety of burlesque houses around the country: the **Trocadero** in Philadelphia, the **Irving Palace** in New York City, the **Old Howard** in Boston, and the **Gayety** in Boston. A few small circuits managed to hang on into the sixties. Skipper and McCaghy (1971) interviewed a number of strippers who were employed by an "eastern wheel" which provided performers for 11 theaters throughout the Midwest. The dancers were required to belong to the American Guild of Variety Artists (AGVA); they were paid

$175 a week plus train fare. Around the same time Marilyn Salutin (1971) interviewed dancers working at a burlesque theater in Canada. These authors report on the difficult work situations of burlesque performers during its death throes. Dirty, smelly theaters, rude and offensive customers, mistreatment by theater managers, poor pay (Salutin's dancers averaged $165 a week) and scant hope of upward mobility made work in burlesque demoralizing.

However, like vaudeville and the minstrel show, burlesque has never completely vanished. Ann Corio toured with **This Was Burlesque** and Dave and Sandy O'Hara Hanson (aka The Improper Bostonian) also toured with a burlesque revue. At one time they brought their revue to a number of condos owned by senior citizens in Florida. The residents were encouraged to play parts in the revue, using costumes furnished by the troupe. Occasionally, Broadway hosts shows built around burlesque, i.e., **Sugar Babies** and **Gypsy**, based on the life of Gypsy Rose Lee and her indomitable mother, Rose. Also burlesque productions on a newly revitalized Coney Island are attracting audiences. The stripper, Dita Von Tease, is currently performing at private parties for celebrities including Elton John and designer Marc Jacobs and is negotiating to star in a burlesque show in Las Vegas.

Mass-mediated Entertainment. Beginning around the turn of the century mass-mediated entertainment began to replace live performance. In 1891 Thomas Edison patented a rudimentary movie camera while the Lumiere brothers in France had also invented a movie camera and opened a movie theater. The first penny arcade opened in New York City in 1894. For a penny a customer could watch a 10 second movie. Another technological development ushered in the nickelodeon, a real movie theater. By 1910 in the United States there were at least 17,000 nickelodeons attended by around 7 million people daily. In 1903 the first full-fledged movie with plot, action, story line and characters, **The Great Train Robbery,** thrilled audiences. By 1914 the feature film **Birth of a Nation** confirmed the dominance of moving pictures over competing entertainment forms.

Many of the early film stars had come from live performance, e.g., Buster Keaton, Charlie Chaplin, Mary Pickford, but they were recognized for their work in pictures. Somewhat later the Broadway star, Al Jolson, talked, or more accurately, sang in the first *talkie,* **The Jazz Singer** in 1927/8. The dominance of silent films ended when Jolson sang.

Almost from the beginning films were about stars. These fortunate few were able to ask for enormous salaries while the rank and file were paid little. Movies gradually replaced playing the **Palace** or starring on Broadway as the pinnacle of show business achievement. The early films made for the nickelodeon did not list the players, but by 1912 most films did more than just identify the cast; producers used mass marketing techniques to promote their stars, including tie-ins with products, still photographs and the encouragement of fandom (deCordova 1991; Gledhill 1991). Mary Pickford was the first movie star and probably the first entertainer recognized by hundreds of thousands of people around the world. It is no wonder that movies continue to be the Holy Grail of show folks.

In 1897 Marconi received a patent for a wireless and started a telegraph company. The first documented voice transmission made by wireless was in 1906. In America commercial radio began with the formation of the Radio Corporation of America in 1919. Until the 1950s with the increased accessibility of television, radio and film operated in tandem. Eddie Cantor, Edgar Bergen, Abbott and Costello, Jack Benny, Bob Hope, Burns and Allen and Al Jolson all had extensive stage careers but were featured in both movies and radio.

Radio and the phonograph changed the direction of popular music. From the early 1880s till WWII the production of popular music was dominated by the songwriters/composers who worked around Tin Pan Alley in New York City. A relatively small number of composers turned out the songs which were disseminated through sheet music. Vaudeville and film stars were used to *plug* the songs.

Beginning in 1899 Louis Glass, the father of the "juke box" put pay phonographs in amusement parks, penny arcades and other venues (Garofalo 1997). The early phonographs were expensive and only the wealthy could own them, but they gradually became more affordable. In the meantime by the 1920s commercial radio was expanding across the country. Musicians and singers became more important to the music industry than the composers, and they used radio and records to expand their audience. The reach and relative cheapness of radio allowed musicians representing various ethnic, racial and regional groups to reach their audiences.

The music publishers' association (ASCAP) charged radio stations large fees to broadcast music; consequently, in the 1930s radio stations boycotted ASCAP and set up their own licensing agency, Broadcast Music Incorporated (BMI) which recruited Black, Hispanic and country and western (c&w) artists for material. The dominance of New York based pop music was broken.

During this period artists followed a variety of paths toward recognition. Some cut their own records and took them to radio stations, begging the station manager for air play. Some artists became disk jockeys to plug their records and live performances. However, a large number of artists were "discovered" by A&R (artists and repertoire) men who went into the field in search of new talent.

Over the last seventy years the recording industry has expanded and contracted. Small labels like Sam Phillips' legendary Sun Records along with such labels as Okeh, Blue Note and Arista have found and developed new artists who are then signed by the major labels. Until the last few years the major labels have held a stranglehold on artists. The labels decide which artists to promote and then spend hundreds of thousands of dollars to build their chosen performers. Those who are not favored are rarely heard from again. With the advent of MTV (Music Television Channel) in 1981 artists and their labels were forced to produce expensive videos which further encouraged labels to promote only a few musicians. In 2003 five global music companies control 85% of the record business while the remaining 15% is divided up between some 10,000 more or less independent labels (Seabrook 2003:45).

However, the ability of labels to control the distribution of their artists' music has been severely hampered by new computer technologies which allow individuals to copy and swap music over the Internet. Currently, the major labels are developing strategies, both legal and technological, to fight this "piracy."

Despite the importance of recordings, the backbone of the music industry continues to be live performance. Generally, an artist only gets around 12% of the retail price of a CD (after the label has deducted all its expenses in producing and marketing the CD). An artist may have a platinum album and receive no money. Artists make money by touring; they get a larger percentage of the ticket sales plus on site sales of CDs, tee shirts and other merchandise.

Currently, the music industry is undergoing rapid change. While the last several years has seen a leveling off of record sales, attendance at concerts continues to grow according to **Pollstar**, an industry trade magazine. Artists are beginning to cut and market their own CDs, thus bypassing the labels. They distribute their CDs at block parties and sell them over the Internet.

The power of artists is challenging the power of the labels; the shift is from the music business to the *musician* business.

Entertainers as culture workers: the Present and Future. On fabled Coney Island **The Coney Island Sideshow** provides traditional sideshow acts like **Eak the Geek** and **Insectavada** to amuse enthusiastic audiences. Strip clubs, live bands, magicians and comics play clubs, street festivals, and fellowship halls. Most of the show people performing in these venues experience the same kind of work environments as did the entertainers of times past: low pay, low prestige and job security plus the necessity of touring. Yet, there are more candidates for show business jobs than there are openings, and many persist through a lifetime of disappointment and penury.

At the other end of the spectrum there are the stars: the singers, comics, musicians and even a few magicians who are famous and command huge fees. The remainder of this book is devoted to a study of the work lives of a sample of entertainers, some famous, a few relatively unknown. Its central focus is to understand this central paradox: why is the supply of entertainers as culture workers greater than the demand? Why do they persist in an occupation in which the chance of success is so slim? Not only in the United States but also in countries like Iraq young people are dreaming, planning and plotting to win talent contests so as to become the next Britney Spears.

The power of the mass media has brought the dream of stardom to every corner of the globe. In the past young people were most often recruited into show business by family members or friends. Often a life in show business was an economic necessity, not a choice. But with the dominance of the mass media the dream of stardom is available to all. In the future live entertainment will persist, and young people will increasingly aspire to join the ranks of show folks.

CHAPTER THREE
SHOW PEOPLE: THE SOCIAL SCIENCE VIEW

Most of us know a little about the early lives of show people; we may have read their autobiographies or seen profiles on television. Yet, social scientists have learned much less about entertainers than other occupational groups such as physicians, nurses or lawyers in spite of their economic and cultural importance. In this chapter I present some of the research on entertainers, organized by speciality. There are five major specialities within the live performance domain: musician, singer, dancer, and comic and variety performer. Some, if not most professional entertainers, have more than one speciality. Fred Astaire was a dancer, singer and actor; Bob Hope sang, danced, told jokes and acted. However, performers are identified with one primary speciality, as, for example, Astaire as a dancer and Hope as a comic.

Entertainer as an occupation. Entertainers are considered a profession by the Bureau of the Census. However, their educational background and employment history bear little resemblance to that of those in the *learned professions*, e.g., medicine, law, dentistry, architecture. Instead entertainers and actors are usually included under the rubric *artistic professions,* together with novelists, composers, and painters. Key descriptive words which identify artists are *originality, creativity, talent and non-conformity* (Florida 2002).

Sociologists have resisted designating entertainers as professionals, but have had difficulty suggesting a category in which they might fit. Wilhelm and Sjoberg (1958:72) in their study of the social background of entertainers argue that:"Entertainers are marginal professionals, for at least two reasons: (1) they tend to flout many of the ideal norms of the total society, and

(2) they have less education than most other professional persons." Florida (2002) calls entertainers part of the "super-creative core" together with those in such industries as broadcasting, video gaming, and film. The position of entertainer in the occupational spectrum is only important to the extent that some sociologists view the choices of show business and professional sports as routes of upward mobility. So the question becomes "do those who choose entertainment improve their social standing relative to that of their parents?"

Efforts to identify and enumerate entertainers are fraught with difficulty for the following reasons:

a) Most self-identified entertainers are frequently unemployed or employed as other than entertainer.
b) The Bureau of the Census, the Department of Labor Statistics and the National Endowment for the Arts collect data on entertainers, but usually merge entertainers with classical artists or non-performers like director or composer.
c) Entertainer labor unions occasionally survey their membership, but most entertainers are not members of labor unions.
d) Anyone can become an entertainer by announcement; hence, individuals move freely and frequently between entertainer self-identification and other occupational self-identifications.

Even though "official statistics" are extremely problematic, they do provide a broad general picture of demographic changes in the entertainment field. The "artistic labor market" is growing (Menger 1999; Alper, Wassali, et.al. 1996; Statistical Abstract 2002). While the ratio of female to male varies over the years and between specialities (musicians are predominately male), females are gradually closing the gap. In 1983 women comprised 42.7% of the category "writers, artists, entertainers and athletes"; currently women comprise 49.7% of the total. Blacks and other minorities are also significantly increasing their participation in both the arts and entertainment. Blacks and other minorities comprised 7.7% of the "writers and entertainers" category in 1983, but today they make up 13.2% of the total (Statistical Abstract 2002).

Unemployment and underemployment are also increasing (Menger 1999). One study commissioned by the American Guild of Variety Artists (AGVA) in 1982 (Ruttenberg et.al.) found that the majority of their members were White males between the ages of 18 and 45. One-third had been unemployed during the previous year. Fully 76% of the dancers, 67% of the actors, 61%

of the singers, and 35% of the musicians were unemployed during 1980. As the authors made clear, employment in entertainment is not crucial to maintaining one's identity as an entertainer:

> Because employment in the performing arts is typically intermittent, performers' professional attachment to the arts cannot be measured simply by the amount of time they work as performers during a given time period. They may consider themselves performing artists even though they worked in their professions very little—or not at all during the year (Ruttenberg et.al. 1982:7).

The euphemism "at liberty" describes the frequent condition of show people— out of work.

Studies of Entertainers' Personalities and Temperamental Characteristics. Psychologists and psychiatrists have studied the personality traits of entertainers. Most of this research is based on actors; however, I will briefly review some of their findings. DeWolf Hopper (1927) said actors ". . . cross the footlights out of egoistic desire to strut before an admiring world. They might like to make a fortune but would willingly starve if given adequate publicity." Psychological profiles suggest that these people are pathological, reinforcing the deviant image of entertainers. Fenichel's (1944) study of actors concluded that they were exhibitionists who attempted to gain security against anxieties associated with the Oedipal complex, while Brown (1940) viewed actors as exhibitionist and narcissistic due to genital or phallic fixation. Using the Minnesota Multiphasic Personality Inventory (MMPI) and comparing actors with a control group Chyatte (1940) concluded that actors were high in psychopathology, femininity, paranoia, depression, hypomania and schizophrenia.

Using the MMPI Taft (1961:344-5) described his findings about the actors he studied:

> The over-riding picture that emerges is of a comparatively under controlled, disorganized personality who is quick to panic. He is sensitive to his environment and interested in artistic activities and social relations without empathizing with other people. He is flexible rather than brittle and responds to his environment in an unconventional, even actively non-conforming manner.

These and other studies (Barr et.al. 1972; Green & Money 1966; Lane 1960) all suggest that actors and entertainers are given to self-aggrandizement, anxiety, and delusional behavior. To what extent these personality characteristics represent psychological predispositions or responses to their work in the culture industry is open to question.

Studies of Entertainers' Social Origins and Demographic Patterns. In 1958 using a sample of magazine profiles, Wilhelm and Sjoberg presented data on the social and family backgrounds of 156 entertainers. They hypothesized that entertainment was a route of upward mobility for show people, particularly for women and racial and religious minorities. Consequently, they provided demographic and family background data on their sample. The majority were male (61.4%), White (only three African-Americans), and Protestant (26.3%); however, information on religious affiliation was missing for 44%, and a substantial number of male entertainers were Jewish (12.5%).They estimated that 56.2% of the entertainers grew up in "poor" families; but, as the authors acknowledged, their sample came of age during the depression. The entertainers' fathers were primarily professionals (31.4%) and craftsmen (17.3%). In their sample of show people 16.7% had less than a high school education, 21.2% had some high school and 30.1% had a high school diploma. Only 16.0% had some college, and 11.3% had a college degree. A large percentage of male (38.6%) and female (71.7) entertainers were divorced at least once.

They concluded that entertainment does offer a route of upward mobility; however, they caution that entertainers seem to be unstable persons from the viewpoint of the ideal norms of American society. Their instability appears related to their social origins and to the fact that they have experienced upward mobility.

Most social science research has focused on one particular speciality, e.g., musician, actor, or one particular sub-speciality like rock musician or stripper. In the following sections, I briefly review some of the research on the various entertainment specialities.

Musician. A small number of studies have examined selected demographic characteristics of musicians. Their findings relate, in part, to the type of musician under investigation. Bands are always in the process of formation and dissolution; high school kids may form a garage band, but most, unlike Bruce Springsteen and the E Street Band, break up. There are thousands of bands that play the bars, small clubs, and honky tonks across the country.

Then there are those who actually sign a recording contract and "cut a record." Only a few of the band leaders and/or lead singers become stars.

Historically, most musicians have been and continue to be men (Denisoff & Bridges 1982; MacLeod 1993; Ruttenberg et.al. 1982; Becker 1952; Faulkner 1971); however, there are increasing opportunities for female musicians (Bayton 1999; Groce & Cooper 1990; Dahl 1984; Keyes 1991; Valdez & Haley 1996). Musicians are, on average, older than performers in other specialities (Ruttenberg et.al. 1982; Denisoff & Bridges 1982; MacLeod 1993). The majority of musicians in the United States and the United Kingdom are White, but the number of African-American and Hispanic performers is increasing (Ruttenberg et.al. 1982; Denisoff & Bridges 1982; Bennett 1980; Faulkner 1971; Keyes 1991). However, Blacks have predominated in a number of musical genres, specifically, blues, jazz, and hip hop. Many Black musical groups like the Prairie View Co-eds are largely unknown and neglected by historians and musicologists (Tucker 1999).

Researchers pay particular attention to the relationship between a musician and his audience. Working musicians range in quality from the "guitar-picker" who knows three cords to the highly trained and accomplished instrumentalist. In some venues, i.e., a jazz club, creativity is valued above all else while in others the musicians are just there to provide background. Musicians are often ignored by their audiences, and they may come to see themselves as non-persons (Frederickson & Rooney 1988; Hesmondhalgh 1998; Mullen 1985). Musicians must resign themselves to playing other people's music in the style dictated by the bandleader or the owner of the venue; thus, playing music becomes "just a job." Appignanesi (1973: 55) reprinted an old satirical "Ten Commandments" for cabaret audiences:

1) Come if possible late so that the guests already there will know that you have something else to do.

5) When everything concerning your material welfare has been looked after, take part—even if at first it is unwillingly—in the artistic presentation. Look upon the presenter with contempt right from the start. He is an ass and, because of that, let him feel you're spiritual superiority.

6) Place your loud interruptions exactly where they don't fit.

9) During acts, use your cutlery and glasses in an unbothered fashion. Their sound does good and replaces the band.

While thousands of bands still perform, increasingly, live musicians are being replaced by technology. For example, night clubs and private parties were major employers of musicians, but now DJs with turntables provide the music. Taped music is even replacing live bands in musical theater. Currently, most musicians maintain their self-identity as musician while actually only performing part-time.

Musicians and other entertainers usually perform in venues where alcohol and illicit drugs are sold and consumed. These same venues offer opportunities for sexual exploration. In such environments one of the chief hazards of working in entertainment is the opportunity to engage in "deviant" behavior. Alcoholism, family breakup and drug addiction are some of the consequences of employment in these venues (Valdez & Halley 1996; Bennett 1980; Dahl 1984).

Singer. Singing and playing instruments are, of course, closely allied. Many artists, e.g., Elton John, Bruce Springsteen, Waylon Jennings, Willie Nelson both play instruments and sing. Usually an artist will be identified primarily as a singer (Elton John, Waylon Jennings) or as a musician (Bob Wills, Chet Atkins). Historically, singing is a speciality in which women have achieved almost numerical parity with men. Whether in groups or as soloists women in diverse cultures have sung professionally (Koskoff 1987; Goldner 1983; Valdez & Halley 1996). Most musical troupes contain at least one female vocalist. Gypsies, Russian and German folk musicians and other troupes understood the value of their female performers in attracting male audiences. The development of polyphonic music in the late middle ages increased the need for female voices to sing the soprano parts. As a result women became integral to the success of both high art like opera and also the popular music of the day.

Female stage performance has always been associated with sexuality and prostitution (Pavletich 1980; Koskoff 1987). Female vocalists and dancers have been characterized as sexual deviants:

> Wife, lover, mother. She is the fallen angel of country, the glamorous fatale of pop, the sassy fox of R& B, the sister of folk. She's a tramp, bitch, and goddess, funky mama, sweetheart, the woman left lonely, the hapless victim of her man (Pavletich 1980:14).

Groce and Cooper (1990) interviewed 15 female Rock and Roll performers, 9 of whom were vocalists. The performers agreed that women enhance the popularity of a band and acknowledged the audience perception that female performers must be "hot stuff." The female performers perceived a pressure to "sell sex" or play upon their sexuality and thus reported feeling objectified by men in the audience (Groce & Cooper 1990: 224).

Singers, whether male or female, are charismatic figures. The *jongleur, troubadour and trouvere were* romantic adventurers who entertained and delighted the nobility (Goldner 1983). Opera stars as well as popular singers have ardent fans. Currently, rock and hip hop stars (vocalists and musicians) are major icons for the young. Dealing with the adulation and their enormous incomes are two of the common career contingencies which have derailed the careers of many of these stars (Friedlander 1996).

The vast majority of band leaders are men, and the vocalists and side men/women work at the pleasure of the leader. Even though many musicians and vocalists view themselves as creative and are eager to develop their own styles and personas, it is the band leader whose "vision" directs the band's sound and style. Some musicians and singers strike out on their own; the majority chooses to remain band singers and musicians.

Dancer. Dancers, like vocalists, were active in most of the troupes that presented entertainments throughout the old and medieval world. In countries as diverse as Japan, China, Spain and India female dancers attracted males. Because of the appeal of female dancers, dancing is second speciality in which women have achieved numerical parity with men.

While many dance styles are performed primarily by men, the development of show girls enhanced the employment of women. As one early choreographer said, "Give me de pretty wimmens... I don't care den for the talent." As previously discussed, the introduction of **The Black Crook** in New York ushered in burlesque and, eventually, nightclub and carnival stripping. There is a surprisingly rich body of social science research on stripping and female impersonation, beginning with the landmark studies of Skipper and McCaghy on burlesque strippers.

Female strippers. These women perform in several different venues, i.e., burlesque theaters, strip clubs and carnival girls' shows. No matter what the venue, the performances are similar. The dancer begins her act dressed and gradually removes her clothing in a seductive manner. Some contemporary strip clubs (often called Gentlemen's Clubs) dispense with the strip; the performers begin almost nude. Every show usually has a star or feature performer (who may tour) and a number of "house" or local women. Becoming a feature stripper has become a lucrative sideline for pornography stars.

Demographically, most strippers are between the ages of 18 and 35; however recent evidence suggests that dancers are getting younger (Ronai 1992). The majority is White and with at least a highschool and often a college education (Boles 1974; Skipper &McCaghy 1971; Prus & Irini 1980; Ronai & Ellis 1989).Minority participation is increasing, and some clubs hire all African-American or Asian dancers. Skipper and McCaghy (1971) found that a majority of the burlesque dancers in their sample self-identified as lesbian. Income varies widely; most dancers depend on tips for their income. A successful dancer may make as much as $500 to $800 a night and that money is generally "tax free."

Strippers have always had difficulty coping with their audience as they are perceived as sexual, deviant, and promiscuous. Burlesque dancers were somewhat protected from enthusiastic or hostile audience members by a stage. In the 1940s, 50s and 60s, nightclub patrons were prohibited from touching the dancers and most dancers limited their contact with customers to the stage. However, with the development of nude dancing, strippers began to dance on tables for tips. Some clubs feature "lap dancing", an even more intimate setting for customer-dancer interaction. Dancers have developed a number of strategies to attract customers as well as manage those who become unruly.

Dancers develop a persona (sultry vamp, sweet innocent, naughty but nice) along with costumes and props to entice customers; a dancer uses eye contact to encourage the customer to feel that she has singled him out and flattery, cajolery and humor to manipulate him into buying dances (Ronai & Ellis 1989). Strip club conversations between patrons and dancers have been characterized as the "counterfeiting of intimacy" where each partner pretends genuine interest and concern with the other (Boles & Garbin 1974b; Enck & Preston 1988; Wood 2000; Brewster 2003; Perruci 2000).

Most dancers realize that they are viewed as deviant by the larger population and have developed a number of strategies to cope with that realization. Many keep their occupation a secret from parents, kin and neighbors; they see themselves as workers and/or entertainers, two valued statuses, and many "condemn the condemners" by pointing to immoral behavior on the part of male customers and hypocritical wives (Boles 1974; Thompson & Harred 1992; Ronai & Cross 1988).

On a superficial level exotic dancers hold a certain amount of power over their male customers by either paying or withholding attention from them; however, the customer really holds the ultimate power as club owners want happy, free-spending customers: "he who holds the purse strings, (Wood 2000)."

Male stripper. In the late 1970s and early 80s male strippers began to make appearances in clubs across the country (Prehn 1983; Dressel & Petersen 1982; Petersen & Dressel 1982). Often strip clubs reserved a few nights during the week for male strip shows, and no male customers were admitted. The male strippers were usually greeted with wild enthusiasm by the women in attendance. The dancers wore elaborate costumes which enhanced their personas. They, seemingly cheerfully, flirted with the women.

Petersen and Dressel interviewed 14 dancers, all but two were White and ranged in age from 18 to 27(David Petersen, personal communication). Most had no previous show business experience and went into stripping for the money. Like their female counterparts they were expected to exploit their sexuality. Irrespective of their sexual orientation they maintained a strong heterosexual persona. They also felt exploited by their customers and, like their female counterparts, they hid their occupation from significant others (Dressel & Petersen 1982).

While some cities host full-time male strip clubs, most cities rely on troupes of dancers who play a circuit. Troupe members are highly competitive and vie with each other for best costumes and dance routines. (Tewksbury 1994). Petersen (personal communication) suggests that the careers of male strippers are shorter than those of female dancers because: a)there are more alternative job opportunities for men; and b) the stigma associated with being a stripper is greater for men than women because stripping is farther removed from the *ideal* male role.

Female impersonator. Female impersonators are biological males who impersonate females as part of a performance. Most impersonators are gay self-identified and perform in gay nightclubs and are often referred to as *drag queens* (Newton 1972; Tewksbury 1993). Cities with a sizeable gay population usually support one or two clubs featuring drag queens or illusionists (as some prefer to be called) while a number of troupes tour.

Tewksbury (1993) interviewed 10 female impersonators, all of whom were White and ranged in age from 22 to 36. Nine were gay-identified; one was bisexual. Nine of the sample had full time day jobs or were in school. Similarly to the male and female strippers, these performers had well-developed personas with co-ordinating costumes and routines. They explained their choice of female impersonation as: ". . . recreation or involvement in the gay community, a means of attracting attention, and a way to initiate an entertainment career (Tewksbury 1993:470)."

These performers believe that they are stigmatized by the mainstream society as well as the gay community. Impersonators or illusionists are frequently verbally harassed and often in physical danger. Yet, in spite of these problems illusionists view themselves as superior to those "more deviant than themselves", i.e., transvestites and transsexuals. In sum, they are *entertainers* and the others are not.

While the research on strippers is extensive, show and exhibition dancers and soloists have been neglected. Davison (1989) and Evans et.al. (1996) each conducted a study of chorus dancers. Davison interviewed 20 members of the touring company of the musical, **Cats,** and Evans and co-authors conducted a survey of physical injuries sustained by 313 members of Broadway productions and touring companies.

The cast of **Cats** was almost evenly divided between men and women, but the dance director who had the responsibility for training and rehearsing the dancers was male. Most of the cast members tried to imbue their character in the show with individuality within the limits of the script. All complained about the limitations that were placed on their artistic freedom, and five said that they intended to develop an independent act so that, in the words of one cast member, "I can express myself and my own vision. I know that sounds pompous, but that's the way I feel (Davison 1989:9)."

In their survey of injuries to dancers Evans and co-authors found that 55% had sustained at least one injury. Female dancers are more likely to have injuries than males; this difference may be explained, in part, by the high heels worn by many of the women. The authors point to the many environmental hazards associated with stage productions such as poor flooring, fog produced for stage effects and poor heating. Dancing, whether in a strip or drag club or a Broadway stage, may be a hazard to your health.

Comic. Comedy has been a fundamental component of all theater from the Greeks to contemporary situation comedies. Comics may work in sketches or on stage alone without props, i.e., stand-up. Some write their own routines while others perform the words written by others. Stand-up is the most high risk comic form. The comic, using neither props or costumes, stands in front of the audience and delivers his monologue. If he doesn't get a laugh in the first two minutes, he loses his audience and exits a failure. Comedy, particularly stand-up, is still largely a White male field, though the numbers of women and minorities are increasing (Janus 1980; Fisher & Fisher 1981; Salutin 1973; Stebbins 1990; Greenbaum 1997). A significant number of comics are Jewish (Fisher & Fisher 1981; Janus 1980).

Several researchers have examined the childhood experiences and personality configurations of comics and have found that: a) they had strong relationships with their mothers; b) they were class clowns in elementary and high school; c) they need to control and dominate their audiences; d) they often started their careers as amateurs and gradually turned professional as they met with audience approval; and e) they use comedy to vent hostility. A recent study of the testosterone levels of men in eight occupations including minister, actor, comic, and football player found that actors and comics had the highest testosterone level (Dabbs, LaRue & Williams 1990). The authors conclude that actors and comics need to assert their dominance over their audiences, and also tend toward self-aggrandizement and "anti-social" tendencies. Comics act as contemporary "fools":

> The oldest, most basic role of the comedian is precisely this role of negative exemplar. The grotesque, the buffoon, the simpleton, the scoundrel, the drunkard, the liar, the coward, the effete, the tightwad, the boor, the egoist, the cuckold, the shrew, the weakling, the neurotic, and other such reifications of socially unacceptable traits are enacted by the comedian to be ridiculed, laughed at, repudiated, and, finally, symbolically 'punished' (Mintz 1985:71-80).

Variety. As discussed in Chapter One, variety originated with the shamans who used magic, ventriloquism, mime, acrobatics, juggling and assorted specialities to enchant and mystify their audiences. Variety is the backbone of show business. The singers or comics may hold center stage, but the show opens with a magician or animal trainer. Variety acts were the staple of vaudeville and television variety shows like Ed Sullivan's **Toast of the Town.**

Over the years most variety acts were small-time though there have been a few headliners, e.g., Edgar Bergen (ventriloquist), Sigfried and Roy (animal trainers), The Great Blackstone (magician). There are few studies of variety artists, but a large number of studies of a few work settings in which variety artists are employed, i.e., the circus and the carnival sideshow.

Most variety artists are male, especially magicians, clowns, ventriloquists and jugglers (Nardi 1988; Peter Rich, personal communication). However, women predominate in such specialities as contortion and acrobatics. Currently, most variety artists are White, but, again, minority participation is increasing (Linde 1992).

Variety performers are generally recruited in one of two ways. Many performers are the children and grandchildren of performers, particularly circus troupes consisting of family members specializing in one or two acts like animal training or clowning (Carmeli 1991; Little 1991). The children apprentice with their parents and are paid professionals at a young age.

However, other variety performers become *enchanted* with a particular speciality and study that skill throughout childhood. A child sees a juggler or magician and wants to emulate him. Books and videos help the youngster learn the skill. Most begin as amateurs and gradually turn professional as they meet with acceptance (Stebbins 1984).Many begin their professional careers as street performers working for tips from passersby. A number of countries, particularly Russia, China and France, provide state-supported training programs for budding variety artists. In the United States Ringling Brothers used to maintain a school for clowns but no longer does so (Sugarman 2000).

While variety artists suffer from the same insecurities as other performers, those that work primarily in outdoor show business, i.e., the circus, medicine show and carnival, are especially vulnerable. Outdoor show business is the bottom of the status hierarchy within entertainment. Street and carnival sideshow performers are usually held in low esteem by their audiences. Like the burlesque comic, the outdoor performer must develop a thick skin and a line of patter to deflect and blunt the verbal and sometimes physical attacks from their audiences (Brouws & Caron 2001; Bogdan 1988; Fiedler 1978).

"If you can play a carnival sideshow, you can play anything, anywhere (Peter Hennen, personal communication).

Even though the research reviewed in this section derives from small, non-random samples, some generalizations are possible.

a) The majority of entertainers are White males; however, the number of female and racial and ethnic minority participants is increasing. Women have reached parity in two specialities, singer and dancer.

b) Most entertainers are frequently unemployed but continue to identify themselves as entertainers.

c) Some research suggests that performers may possess personality characteristics which push them toward choosing show business.

d) Some performers are the children of performers and learn through childhood apprenticeship. Many performers begin their careers as amateurs or street performers.

e) Entertainers have a problematic relationship with their audiences. They are vulnerable to any signs of disapproval and may develop hostility toward audiences. Conversely, they hunger for audience approval.

f) Almost without exception entertainers are forced to tour; consequently, they are freed from the normative structures of settled communities. Also, they perform in venues which facilitate deviant behavior.

This literature review points to the lack of data on entertainers: their demographic and family background characteristics, their career trajectories, and the dynamics of the interactions between performers and audience. The central purpose of this book is to expand our understanding of this key component of the culture industry, live popular performance. A study of the biographies of entertainers will contribute to this understanding.

Chapter Four

THE SOCIAL AND DEMOGRAPHIC CHARACTERISTICS OF SHOW PEOPLE

In this chapter I present the social-demographic backgrounds of the entertainers in the sample. Before proceeding, I briefly describe the processes by which the sample was drawn and the data analyzed.

Research Methods

Sampling Biographies. As the two central research questions are: why do people choose entertainment and why do they persist, I required a data source that would provide rich descriptions of the life histories of entertainers. I elected to use biographies and autobiographies. Biographies provide important sources of life history data (Shumaker 1999). Biographies of entertainers are in abundant supply. The public seemingly has an insatiable appetite for reading about the intimate lives of their favorite stars, and the same stars are rarely hesitant about seeing their names in print. There is an apocryphal story that show people tell: two entertainers run into each other:

> 1st entertainer: Harry, good to see you. Did I tell you what happened? I've got my new TV show. I just finished standing room only in Vegas. I'm guesting on the **Tonight** show. Okay, enough about me, let's talk about you. What do you hear about me?

Entertainers write (or hire a ghostwriter) their autobiographies, or authorize a biography. Occasionally, unauthorized biographies are produced, sometimes by scholars or by writers seeking to make money by "exposing" a popular figure. Show people do not always tell the truth, or, put another way, know how to tell a good story. And, like all of us, they are eager to be shown in a positive light. Consequently, using biographies and autobiographies of show people is risky. Self-constructed autobiographies and biographies are called "press releases" and may contain both *true facts* and *narrative truth* (Wiersma 1988). Both *truths* can be unearthed by careful attention to the text. A full length text provides a wealth of rich data about the career contingencies and life experiences of its subject. Show business biographies allow the reader access to the decision-making processes of the entertainers as they meet the challenges inherent in a career in the culture industry.

Theoretical Perspectives and Sensitizing Concepts. My approach to the study of entertainers derives from my research on strippers as well as personal experiences as both an observer and participant in show business. The work of Robert Stebbins has been particularly influential in guiding my approach to studying entertainers. Stebbins (1992) describes four career stages: beginning, development, establishment and decline. I use this scheme in organizing the career contingencies of performers over the life span. Further, I use a number of concepts from the *sociology of work* perspective in guiding my analyses. I examine occupational choice, socialization and career contingencies of the sample with a view toward explicating the processes by which they first choose and then become committed to entertainment.

For the chapter on *motivation* I rely on the research on social motivation derived from the work of David McClelland and others. Using a coding system devised by David Winter I coded the autobiographies for three social motives, achievement, affiliation and power. The results of that analysis and the implications I have drawn are presented with a view toward explicating the relationship between motive predispositions and work experiences.

Selecting the Sample. The data on which the remaining chapters of this book are based consist of 117 biographies and autobiographies of entertainers. In selecting the books in the sample I sought to include:

> a) performers who were active from around the 1850s to the present. Modern show business emerged in the 1850s but has evolved over the years due to changes in technology, cultural attitudes and values, and the organizational structure of show business. Further, I wanted to document any changes in the social-demographic composition of show people over the years.
> b) entertainers from all five of the specialities. Biographies of singers and musicians far outnumber those of other specialities, especially variety artists.
> c) largely unknown performers as well as those who were famous.

In an effort to achieve those goals, I developed a theoretical sampling strategy (Strauss & Corbin 1998) which began with a collection of book titles of entertainers derived from a number of sources and were collated into a master list of over 400 titles. From this list I largely eliminated biographies of the foreign born. I solicited copies of autobiographies of little known entertainers that were privately printed.

Eventually, I had a master list of 205 biographies of entertainers spanning over a hundred years. I eliminated duplications as some performers like Elvis Presley were profiled more than once. I also eliminated titles that appeared to be insufficiently developed for my purpose. Comics, for example, are prone to write autobiographies which are essentially collections of amusing anecdotes. I then categorized the books by birth date and speciality of the subject. Based upon changes in society and the entertainment industry I divided the entertainers into three birth cohorts: 1850-1920 (T1), 1921-1940 (T2) and 1941 to the present (T3).

In choosing books for the sample, I attempted to include an approximately equal number of titles from each time period, entertainers from all five specialities and a significant number of entertainers who are largely unknown. My master list now comprised 191 books. From this I chose a random sample of 109 books. To this sample I added three titles about little-known performers, and an additional four titles from the third time period and an additional title about a variety performer. My final sample comprised 117 books, 67 were biographies, the remaining 50 autobiographies. Forty-four artists were born during T1, 33 during T2, and 40 during T3.

Coding. Prior to reading the biographies I conducted in-depth interviews with two performers, one retired and one still performing. I used a very open format, relying on Stebbins' career stages to elicit responses about their careers over the life span. I conducted a line-by-line coding of these texts looking for key events which precipitated changes in career trajectories. Also, I carefully noted material presented with a high affect. Using the insights developed from these interviews as well as concepts derived from *sociology of work* research, I developed a code book, a copy of which may be requested to this author.

The primary function of the code sheet was to record *true facts,* that is, information about the timing of key events in the performers' lives, e.g., first performing job, acquiring an agent.

Beyond the coding of specific information, I searched and collected passages from the texts which dealt with *narrative truth,* such as: relations with audiences, rewards of entertainment, disappointment and rejection, changes in career plans or directions. I grouped responses to the same or similar issues (for example, fear of failure or reaction to first audition) and cross-compared those responses across the sample. Of particular importance were narratives connected to strong affect. Both similarities and differences between individuals were noted. I focused on examining these findings in terms of the key categories of entertainers: unknown/famous, birth cohort, speciality, race/ethnicity, religion, and gender.

In the following section, I present the data on the social demographic characteristics of entertainers by birth cohort.

WHO ARE ENTERTAINERS?

Regretfully, biographies are not written for the convenience of sociologists. Crucial information is often missing, occasionally, even birth date. However, missing information most often includes education and occupation of mother, education of father, educational attainment of the subject, and extent of religious participation in the family of origin. In some cases I have made inferences on the family background of the performers based on the texts. For example, if the mother is never shown working outside the home, I have inferred that she was a housewife.

Racial categorization was often difficult to decipher. Some entertainers came from mixed racial backgrounds but self-identified with one race. It wasn't until the most recent time period (T3) that entertainers began to self-identify as bi-racial. In categorizing the show people by race I relied on their self-identifications. Two entertainer self-identified as transgendered; one identified as a transsexual and the other as a transvestite.

Gender and Ethnicity. Similarly to other studies, the majority of this sample was males; 69.4% were males, 30.3% females and two were transgendered. Almost 70% (69.1%) were White, 26% Black, and 4.9% were of mixed race. The predominance of White males is striking; however, when the data are disaggregated by birth cohort, significant changes emerge.

Table 1											
Percent Gender and Race/Ethnicity by Birth Cohort											
Birth Cohort											
	Pre 1900-1920			1921-1940			1941- Present			Total		
	M	F	T	M	F	T	M	F	T	M	F	T
	(n = 44)			(n = 33)			(n = 40)			(n = 117)		
Race												
White	63.6	9.1	2.2	48.5	21.2	0	35.0	30.0	0	49.0	21.1	0.32
Black	20.5	4.5	0	21.2	9.1	0	12.5	10.0	2.5	19.1	7.9	0.38
Mixed	0	0	0	0	0	0	5.0	5.0	0	2.2	2.3	0

The percent of each race and gender total 100% for all nine cells within each Birth Cohort, thus 63% of the first cohort in Pre 100-1920 are White Males.

The percent of White male performers falls from a high of 63.6% in T1 to 35% in T3. The percent of White females rises over the same period from 9.1% to 30%. Yet, the percent of Black male performers holds steady for two periods, and then drops significantly in T3(12.5%). However, the percent of Black female performers rises slowly from 4.5% in T1 to 10% in T3. Four performers in T3 self-identified as having a mixed racial heritage.

What accounts for the precipitous drop in Black male performers over the span of this study? In public perception Blacks, especially Black males, are associated with blues and jazz. The great Black musicians, singers and composers burst on the scene in the 1920s and 30s, Duke Ellington, Earl Hines, Eubie Blake and Fats Waller among many. The lives of these early *greats* have been extensively profiled. With the end of WWII folk and rock music became popular, both dominated by White musicians. Recently, hip hop/ rap music has become popular so in the future we can expect an increase in biographies of these artists. A few African American comics, Richard Pryor and Bill Cosby in particular, paved the way for the acceptance of films and television shows featuring Black comics, many of whom will be profiled in the future. A number of performers had a Latino heritage: Joan Baez, Freddie Prinze, Ricky Martin and Mariah Carey. I expect to see an increase in Latino performers, and, consequently, more biographies.

Religion. Religious background was mentioned in only 72.7% of the biographies. Of those whose religious heritage could be ascertained, a quarter (25.1%) were raised Catholic, 50.5% Protestant, and 24.4% Jewish With the exception of T2 the percentage of those reared in the three primary religions held relatively steady. While the percent of Catholics and Protestants reflects their relative distribution in the general population, the percent raised in the Jewish faith far outstrips their numbers in the population. Jews have been and continue to be strongly represented as singers and comics: Eddie Fisher, Al Jolson, Jerry Lewis, Chico Marx, Gilda Radner, Joan Rivers, Jack Benny, Milton Berle, Fanny Brice, to name a few. The prominence of Jewish comics has been attributed to the importance of ethnic humor in vaudeville. Jewish people were largely urban and eager audiences. Non-Jews came to appreciate "Jewish" humor. However, Janus (1980) argues that most Jewish humor deals in Jewish stereotypes which comics trade on, thereby easing the concerns of their Jewish audiences by encouraging them to laugh at those stereotypes while, perhaps, reinforcing these stereotypes among Gentiles.

Participation in churches and synagogues was extremely important in the lives of many of the show people. Four were children of preachers: Sam Kinison, Nat Cole, Darlene Love and Sam Cooke, and Al Jolson's father was a cantor. Many were raised in strongly religious homes and gained their first performing experiences in churches or synagogues. Darlene Love, Sam Cooke, Jerry Lee Lewis, Snoop Dogg, Tammy Wynette, and Whitney Houston first learned they could sing in church. Darlene Love said that so many singers got their start in church choirs that they operated as "farm teams" for the recording companies.

Approximately one half of the Protestant entertainers' families belonged to holiness or fundamentalist denominations; two were Jehovah's Witnesses. Though their services differ, these denominations stress the inerrancy of the Bible. They view alcohol use and sex outside of marriage as sins. Church attendance is a significant part of their lives. Children are taught that secular music and dancing almost inevitably lead to drunkenness and sexual promiscuity. The majority of the entertainers raised in these denominations were warned against and often forbidden to play secular music and perform in venues outside the church.

For those raised in such a faith, the lure of secular music and public performance was set against the prohibitions of the church. The biographies record the extreme discomfort these entertainers felt as they began to pull away from the church. Some, like Sam Cooke, gradually drifted from singing gospel to popular music. The majority like Jerry Lee Lewis and Waylon Jennings split with the church fairly early in their careers. For some guilt feelings remained throughout their lives; while for others, they managed to reconcile their chosen career with their childhood faith. For example, Sam Cooke's father came to accept his son's turn toward popular music.

Those who seemingly emancipated themselves adopted one of two strategies. Five demonized their religion. The religious denomination itself was at fault; its beliefs were wrong-headed, narrow-minded and life destroying. The second, more popular solution was to view their performances as providing pleasure, spiritual uplift, joy, and harmony to audiences. They were using their *god-given talents (the gift)* to improve others' lives.

Educational Attainment of the Sample. Educational attainment was coded less than high school, high school graduate and education beyond high school. As seen in Table 2 overall half (54.7%) of the sample had less than high school, while almost 20% had some formal education beyond high school. Eddie Heywood left school at age eight; Bob Wills quit school in the 7th grade, and probably W. C. Fields and Howard Thurston never went beyond the fifth grade. Jim Morrison, Dinah Shore, Bill Cosby and Rudy Vallee were all college graduates. Heidi Mattson, the "Ivy League Stripper" parlayed her attendance at Brown University into a book and a number of television appearances.

Table 2
Percent Educational Attainment by Birth Cohort

	1850-1920	1921-1940	1941 - Present	Total
Education	(n = 44)	(n = 33)	(n = 40)	(n =117)
Less than High School	77.3	57.6	27.5	54.7
High School Graduate	6.8	27.3	45.0	25.6
Education Beyond High School	15.9	15.2	27.5	19.7

Educational attainment of the sample increased dramatically over the last 100 years. While the percent of those with less than high school decreased, the percent of high school graduates and college attendees increased, reflecting the increase in educational attainment of Americans as a whole.

Some performers were encouraged and/or pressured to continue their schooling, others were not so encouraged. Often the children had to work to help support their families. Those who could earn money performing were strongly motivated to do so. Performing was preferred over picking cotton, bussing tables, or working in the mills. As Milton Berle (p.53) said:

> I guess I thought my childhood was fun while I was living it. Looking back, I can feel in my gut that it was lousy. Pa had no talent for supporting a family, and mama had to take over. She had seven Berlingers to keep alive and together.

Berle, like many others became the financial mainstay of his family while still a child.

Family of Origin's Social and Economic Status. As adults the vast majority of the entertainers made much more money than their parents. They lived in enormous houses, drove luxury cars and carried entourages. In a word they lived *large*. Certainly, the possibility of immense wealth is one of the considerations for those who choose entertainment.

Sociologists use father's occupation as an indicator of family socioeconomic status, together with income and education. In this study, I identified the primary occupation of the entertainers' fathers (or step-fathers) and mothers. Father's occupation was coded as show business, professional, white collar, blue collar, farmer, military, and other/unemployed. These were combined into white collar/professional, blue collar, farmer and entertainer. The "entertainer" category was stretched a bit to include closely related jobs. For mother's occupation I used the same coding scheme except I added housewife.

Coding father's occupation was complicated. Sometimes only hints were given—"my dad had a college education and a really good job." Often the father held a variety of jobs; for example, one was ostensibly a farmer but was actually a bootlegger.

Most mothers were homemakers; yet, many supplemented the families' incomes as part-time workers, e.g., seamstresses, servants, and the like. I will include those mothers' occupations which are important to the childhoods of the sample.

In the first birth cohort 56.8% of the fathers held blue collar jobs while five (11.4%) had show business backgrounds. Eddie Heywood's father was a trained pianist who accompanied silent films. Georgia Sothern's father abandoned her as an infant, but she was apprenticed in show business by her uncle beginning at age three. Liberace's father, who mightily disapproved of his son's choice of music, was a musician with John Philip Sousa's band. Billie Holliday's father was a guitarist, but as a child, she had little contact with him. Red Skelton's father was a vaudeville performer.

Table 3			
Percent Occupational Attainment of Entertainment Fathers by Birth Cohort			
Birth Cohort			
Occupation	1850 -1920	1921-1940	1941 - Present
	(n = 44)	(n = 33)	(n = 40)
White Collar/ Professional	25.0	21.2	32.5
Blue Collar	56.8	45.5	50.0
Farmer, Military and Other	6.8	12.1	7.5
Show Business	11.4	21.2	10.0

For the second cohort less than half (45.5%) of the fathers were blue collar workers, but the percent of those in show business rose to 21.2%. Sammy Davis, Jr., began performing with his father and "uncle" when he was three. Doris Day's father was a church organist and choral director. Judy Collins' father, though blind, hosted a popular radio show in which he sang, read poetry and philosophized. Phyllis Newman's mother and father were both performers. Her mother, aka Marvelle, read palms. Her father was called either Dr. S. A. Newman or Gabel the Graphologist. He also accompanied Phyllis when she began performing at age six. Though Gunther Gebel-Williams' father was not strictly an entertainer, he built sets for theaters so young Gunther was around show people as a child. Lenny Bruce's mother was an eccentric dancer and later ran a school for strippers. As a child Patsy Cline sang gospel with her mother.

In the third cohort one half (50.5%) of the fathers were blue collar workers while 10% were in show business. Prince's and Jim Carrey's fathers were both musicians, at least during part of their work lives. Barbara Mandrell's father was a policeman but also a musician who was influential in developing her career. Jett Williams' father was the legendary Hank Williams; however, she did not discover her paternity until adulthood. While not in show business, Reba McEntire's father was a rodeo star, and Reba began her career singing in rodeos.

Mariah Carey's mother was an opera singer and trained young Mariah in opera. Garth Brooks' mother was a country singer, and Whitney Houston's mother was the well known gospel singer, Cissy Houston.

"We were so poor that"… jokes are a staple of most comics' routines:

> I grew up in an apartment that was so bad, they tore it down to build a tenement.
>
> We were so poor even our rats had to take in roomers.
>
> I was so poor I couldn't even afford to have my own dreams.

More humor and sympathy can be gained from audiences by "poor" rather than "rich" jokes ("We were so rich even our mice ate with sterling silver"). However, the biographies suggest that most entertainers' family incomes were similar to others in their communities. Yet, in each cohort a few were significantly different from the norm. In T1 Will Rogers, Rudy Vallee, Ethel Merman and Dinah Shore had well-to-do parents. Some grew up in abject poverty: Billie Holiday, Woody Guthrie, Augustus Rapp, George Burns, Fats Waller. Augustus Rapp's account of his early childhood provides a flavor of the experience of extreme poverty.

> Food was scarce. The attic housed about two hundred pigeons. When the rats need food, they pillaged the nest and ate the young pigeons. When my parents needed food, they ate the older pigeons. I did not inherit any genes of value from my parents as pa worked on the river boat which bootlegged whiskey and ma slung hash in a cheap restaurant (p.14).

Two performers, W. C. Fields and Howard Thurston left home when they were nine years old. Fields' father was a peddler; no one is sure what Thurston's father did, nor is there any certainty why both ran away. On their own from age nine, both had perilous childhoods. Evidently, Thurston left home with some "potato peelers" and 25 cents his father gave him saying, "Never let it be said that your father didn't give you money for a start."

In the second cohort only two entertainers came from affluent homes: Joan Rivers and John Phillips. None were raised in abject poverty though Etta James, Loretta Lynn, B.B. King and Richard Pryor certainly experienced hunger as children.

The parents in T3 were an interesting contrast. A few had fathers who were high achieving: Ricky Martin, Jim Morrison and Joan Baez. Several fathers were largely absent. Eminem refers to himself as "trailer trash" as he and his mom moved among kin from trailer park to trailer park. Tupac Shakur was strongly influenced by his step-father, Dr. Mutulu Shakur, who was sentenced to prison for conspiring to commit armed robbery and murder. Queen Latifah's role model was her mother, an educator who won many awards for innovative programs directed toward inner city children.

Composition of Family of Origin. The childhoods of entertainers present vivid contrasts. Some like Doris Day grew up in stable, middle class homes, while others were raised in chaos. David Brenner and Loretta Lynn detailed their very positive experiences with their families while others like Tempest Storm dwell on childhood deprivations and trauma.

Family composition was coded intact family with biological father and mother, or one biological parent and one step-parent, with mother or father only and chaotic. Families were coded as chaotic if the entertainer lived with a variety of kin, in orphanages or on the street.

Table 4 Percent Family Composition by Birth Cohort				
Birth Cohort				
Family Composition	1850 -1920	1921-1940	1941 - Present	Total
	(n = 44)	(n = 33)	(n = 40)	(n = 117)
Intact Mom/Dad or 1 Step Parent	68.2	66.7	75.0	70.1
Single Parent	15.9	15.2	15.0	15.4
Chaotic	15.9	18.2	10.0	14.5

The majority of the sample spent their childhoods in intact families (see Table 4). In all three cohorts over 60% grew up in a family composed of their biological parents, or, with one step-parent. Only a small percentage lived in truly harrowing circumstances. Woody Guthrie's mother was mentally ill (Huntington's chorea) and, at one time, set fire to his sister, killing her. As previously noted both W. C. Fields and Howard Thurston ran away from home at age nine. After leaving home Thurston worked as a jockey and bellboy and sold newspapers. At 16 he was convicted as a pickpocket and sentenced to a "reform school." He converted to Christianity and entered divinity school founded by the well-known evangelist, Dwight Moody. He eventually "found" magic instead.

Billie Holiday was the daughter of an unwed mother and a musical, albeit largely absent, father. She was raped when she was ten and arrested for delinquency (truancy, prostitution) and spent a year in a Catholic reformatory. Tupac Shakur's mother, Alfenia, was a prominent Black Panther who successfully defended herself against federal charges; yet, she began to use crack cocaine and live with a physically abusive man. Unable to tolerate this situation, Shakur moved to California to live with relatives.

Woody Guthrie, Willie Nelson, Augustus Rapp, and Jimmie Rodgers spent most of their childhoods in orphanages, foster homes or with kin. As mentioned Eminem and his mother boarded frequently with kin. Gunther Gebel-Williams' father was an alcoholic and beat his mother who, in turn, beat him. Gunther grew up in Germany during the height of WWII. His father went into the army and his mother fed him and his sister by exchanging her sewing for food. His mother was raped by Russian occupiers. The Russians gave young Gunther vodka, and by age ten he had a serious alcohol problem. Finally, when he was 13, Gunther was "sold" to *Circus William* by his parents.

In several cases the performers developed early strong attachments to one parent. Frank Sinatra, Houdini, Fats Waller, Al Jolson, George Burns and Jackie Gleason were among those strongly attached to their mothers. It is believed that Al Jolson never recovered from his mother's untimely death, and his famous rendition of **Mammy** is a tribute to her.

Fanny Brice adored her charming but unreliable father for whom she began performing at an early age. Billie Holiday loved her itinerant, musician father, and at least one biographer (O'Meally 1991) suggested that Holiday's attraction to "bad" men was related to her feelings for her father. Duke Ellington's father was a butler, and the Duke's sense of style was derived from early lessons in dress and decorum. Sam Kinison and his brothers adored their preacher/father and tried to follow in his footsteps. Both Milton Berle and the Marx Brothers had strong mothers who guided and prodded their careers.

Several had alcoholic or drug-using parents including John Phillips, Janis Joplin, Louie Anderson, Augustus Rapp, Jim Carrey, Gunther Gebel-Williams and George Jones. Almost 11% of the sample was physically abused as children, less than 5% reported sexual abuse. Nat Cole was physically abused by his father, and Patsy Cline was a victim of incest. Melissa Etheridge's older sister forced Melissa to masturbate her. Tempest Storm was gang raped when she was in the 8th grade, and her step-father tried to rape her. She ran away from home while still in high school.

Throughout history the physically handicapped have gravitated to show business (see Chapter I). Venues like carnivals and circuses provide safe havens as well as employment for those with disabilities, and some performers have succeeded either in spite of or because of their disabilities.

Only 8.8% of the performers reported any kind of physical disability; however, those who were disabled experienced great emotional pain. Jim Rose, in his autobiography, **Freak Like Me,** wrote about his crossed eyes:

> Given the geriatric population, the kids, even the little kids, in Phoenix had seen a lot: a cane, a wheelchair, a colostomy bag or two. But crossed eyes, my cross to bear—now those were a rarity. I might as well have had two heads with the reaction I triggered. Their doubletakes looked like quadruple to me. My peers would take one glance, start screaming and bolt. Little children pointed at me and clung to their mother's skirt, sobbing. I was a monster (p.28).

Mel Tillis and B.B. King stuttered; Gilda Radner, Louie Anderson, Joan Rivers, Jackie Gleason, Etta James and Fats Waller were overweight. Prince was unusually short. Hedy Jo Starr, who began cross-dressing as a child, owned, operated and stared in carnival girls shows for most of her career. Lady Chablis realized early in life that she was "different" from other little boys; she liked to dress up in women's clothing. Both Starr and Chablis escaped the rejection they found at home in show business, Hedy Jo in carnivals and Lady Chablis in drag shows. As Hedy Jo recalled:

> The kootch {girls show} saved my life. If I hadn't found my way to the midway, I probably would have done myself in. I was that miserable. The carnival was a home, a refuge. Carnies were my family. (personal communication).

In Sum. Over the past 100 years the demographic profile of live performers has shifted. Even though White men still dominate, the percentage of White and Black women has increased. Though still relatively small, the percent of Hispanic performers is increasing. More entertainers are identifying themselves as mixed race.

As would be expected the educational level and occupational attainment of entertainers' parents have increased as has the entertainers' educational attainment. A substantial minority are themselves the children of entertainers. A small minority of the sample were raised in wealthy homes while a substantial percent grew up in very poor homes. The majority were raised in stable families.

Religious affiliation and participation are key factors in the lives of a significant number of the sample. A large percent of singers and comics were Jewish; children raised in Holiness churches also became entertainers, primarily singers and musicians. With the exception of Al Jolson (His father strongly opposed his singing secular music) the Jewish tradition seemed to be supportive of the aspirations of the budding performers. A number of Jewish entertainment enclaves like the Catskills and Miami Beach offered employment and encouragement to beginners. In contrast, the Holiness tradition was not supportive of secular ambitions. Though many performers leaned to sing in church choirs, their *abandonment* of sacred for secular music led to friction with parents and neighbors and, in some cases, feelings of life-long guilt.

The family backgrounds of the Black and White performers were similar. Most were raised in relatively poor but stable homes. Children were expected to help support the family, and the young entertainers began performing for money as a way of supporting their families. The humiliations associated with segregation often came later in the Black performers' careers as they tried to find accommodations in segregated communities or get bookings in more prestigious and better-paying venues.

Except for those raised in show business families or with "stage mothers", the family backgrounds of the entertainers are probably not significantly different from the majority of families living in each cohort. Why then did these individuals choose show business? In the following chapter we look at the beginning career stage when the budding performers begin their long trek on the road to fame and fortune. Some started when they were three years old; most had already been performing for money before they finished high school.

CHAPTER FIVE
LET ME ENTERTAIN YOU: CHOOSING TO ENTERTAIN

The popular comic, Rodney Dangerfield, explained why thousands of, otherwise sane people, choose to become professional entertainers:

> People in show business have this endless desire to be told over and over how wonderful they are. And that desire drives them to perform before the public . . . There are probably more people with more talent outside show business than in. But the outsiders don't have the need to be loved that the insiders do. (Passman 1971:47).

This and the following two chapters encompass the beginning and development stages of Stebbins' career model. This chapter focuses on the processes by which entertainers came to choose that occupation over other options. Our understandings of the choice process are enhanced by using three concepts fundamental to the study of career: predisposing conditions, situational contingencies, and turning points.

Predisposing conditions. Specific characteristics of individuals may predispose them toward certain occupations or inhibit them from choosing them (Boles & Garbin 1974a). The childhoods of most of the sample provide data on both the physical and emotional conditions which predisposed them toward live performance. Two key predisposing conditions present themselves: a sense of differentness and early recognition of performing talent or skill.

A sense of differentness. Most children long to belong—to family, kin and community. The sources of feelings of estrangement are varied; however, three key ones are real or imagined physical differences, emotional estrangement and psychic disengagement.

Physical appearance and ability are key factors in the self concept of children. Physical handicaps or unattractive physical features affect how young children see themselves in relation to significant others. As previously noted a few show people had physical handicaps: Mel Tillis and B.B. King stuttered, and Jim Rose had crossed eyes. Additionally, eight were significantly overweight; of the eight six were comics. Entertaining offered children with physical handicaps a way to cope with isolation, humiliation and shame by amusing others. Louie Anderson learned early that he could use his weight to make others laugh:

> I was in kindergarten, and the teacher was showing the class a new toy someone had donated. It was a white milk truck that could be ridden around the room. All of us stood in line, waiting our turn to drive it around the room . . . Then my turn came. But as I swung my leg over the seat, a little girl screamed, 'Hey, you can't go on the truck! You're too fat. You'll break it.' Several of the kids laughed. Already my weight was generating laughs (p.83).

Joan Rivers found that comedy is an effective tool for "punishing" tormentors:

> Comedy . . . is a medium of revenge. We can deflate and punish the pomposity and the rejection which hurt us. Comedy is power. The only weapon more formidable than humor is a gun (p.23-4).

All the entertainers who had physical disabilities as children incorporated their experiences with these problems into their acts, most especially the comics.

Alcoholic parents, emotional neglect, physical or sexual abuse contributed to feelings of estrangement and isolation for many in the sample. Some like Nat Cole and Dennis Wilson were physically abused; Patsy Cline was a victim of incest; Billie Holiday and Tempest Storm were raped; as a child, Melissa Etheridge was forced to masturbate her older sister. Many lost their parents through death or separation: Al Jolson, Billie Holiday, Tupac Shakur, Snoop Dogg, Fred Allen, B.B. King, Gunther Gebel-Williams, Etta James, Jett Williams, Norma Miller, George Burns, and Georgia Sothern. Woody

Guthrie's mother suffered from a severe mental illness. Alcohol abuse plagued the parents of Jim Carrey, Janis Joplin, John Phillips, among others.

Additionally, a significant number of performers experienced a psychic estrangement from their parents and kin. The sources of this estrangement are primarily two-fold. Even though many in the sample came from economically marginal families, they did not seem to resent (or did not express their resentment) at being "poor." However, a few clearly resented their parents' economic position and early-on were seeking a route of upward mobility. Heidi Mattson whose father was a janitor clearly aspired to a better life. She enrolled in Brown University but then ran into financial difficulties. She decided to become a stripper and capitalize on her status as a student at an Ivy League college; she became "The Ivy League Stripper":

> It was not a desperate act that transformed me from mild-mannered Maine girl into a professional tease. It was a decision. Rational, practical, honest and up-front—a methodical exploration of an option (p.16).

A second performer who linked his choice of occupation to his desire to escape poverty was the comic, David Brenner:

> At the age when most children daydream about being a fireman, policeman, or baseball player, I used to lie in bed at night, daydreaming about my escape from the sweltering heat of my non-air-conditioned room. I saw pictures of the future, my future, wonderful pictures I had played over and over in my mind with one central character, an adult me, all grown up, successful, wealthy, sharing my achievement and money with my family in a hundred different joyful situations (p. 183-4).

Some performers grew up always feeling like "a fish out of water", that is, different from family, kin and neighbors. They found the values and lifestyles of their families stifling. As previously mentioned, many came from very religious homes: Jerry Lee Lewis, Sam Kinison, Nat Cole, Darlene Love, and Waylon Jennings. Travis Tritt, Howard Thurston, W. C. Fields, Melissa Etheridge, Eminem, John Phillips, Jim Morrison, and Janis Joplin all exhibited strong feelings of disengagement with their families of origin. At 14 Janis Joplin began viewing herself as an outsider in conservative Port Arthur, Texas. Being popular with boys was everything to teenage girls, and Janis wasn't. She developed a "tough chick" persona and was labeled the school slut. Throughout her life she exhibited cycles of rebellion and conformity.

61

The two transgendered performers, Lady Chablis and Hedy Jo Starr, recognized their differentness as young children.

> My first good memories are of dressing up in women's clothes. I didn't know I should not be doing that. My mother would get furious. By the time I was five, I knew I was different, and that I would always be different. I knew I would have to find another life because I couldn't live my life at home (Hedy Jo Starr, personal communication).

Many youngsters feel estranged from family and community but become lawyers or plumbers. The major difference between them and the performers is that entertainers discovered early on that they could mesmerize an audience. Once discovered, never forgotten. As Melissa Etheridge said about her first performance:

> I walked off the stage and it was the most connected I'd ever felt in my entire life. Connected to heart. Connected to want. Connected to experience. It was like a drug. A drug made me alive (p.19).

Early recognition of an entertainment talent or skill. A successful showman needs two qualities: a performance skill (singing) and charisma (ability to hold an audience). The vast majority of the sample discovered their skills in childhood; 78% had amateur experience, appearing in school productions, church choirs or local amateur contests. A third (31.7%) had performed on the street, doing magic tricks, picking a guitar, or otherwise entertaining passersby. Will Smith perfected his rap music on the street: "My reputation came from beating other rappers in street challenges. I never lost a street battle (p. 15)." Whether as an amateur or hired performer (83% had received pay for performing before age 14), the majority found they had a performance skill and could hold an audience before they reached their 14th birthday.

By age ten Liberace was playing the piano in a variety of venues from Polish weddings to cabarets. Oliver Hardy toured with a minstrel show when he was eight. Snoop Dogg won rapping contests when he was three, the same age as Jim Carrey when he began imitating **The Three Stooges** at home and at school. Travis Tritt was hooked on performing when he received a standing ovation from his church (Assembly of God) at four. Ricky Martin began his singing career at age six; Buddy Holly won $5 in an amateur contest when he was eight. Eddie Heywood played piano professionally by age eight while Fred Astaire began his professional dance career at four.

> Al Jolson's career began in the summer of 1896 when the Joelson boys became street entertainers at the urging of their friends.
>
> They spent the early evenings singing for congressmen and other high officials who sat on the veranda in front of the Hotel Raleigh, sipping cool drinks. These informal performances gave Al Jolson his first taste of applause, and the indescribable thrill of knowing he had pleased his listeners (p. 16).

Situational contingencies. Most novice show folks take a number of detours before they finally settle on show business. Some were discouraged by parents, others by the roadblocks set in their path. Often the men married young and were hampered by family responsibilities in their quest for a show business career. Women performers like Loretta Lynn and Tammy Wynette had childcare responsibilities which hindered their ability to tour. Situational contingencies are unplanned occurrences which help set a career entry. These events convince the novice to continue to pursue "the dream" in spite of objections of others and the disappointments that are inevitably part of the process of establishing oneself. There are two situational contingencies: seeing the ideal performer and early psychic rewards associated with performing.

Seeing the ideal performer. Slightly over 70% of the show people reported seeing a performer which convinced them "I want to do that." Sometimes the novice is transported by the performance skill, others by the professional's ability to captivate and hold an audience. Bud Freeman was mesmerized by hearing some of the early jazz musicians, including Bix Beiderbecke, and Jimmy McPartland. When he was ten, Bill Boley, the magician and ventriloquist (vent) saw a magician at a school assembly program and determined that he, too, would become a magician. He sent for a magic catalog, ordered a ventrillo and began his magic and vent career.

Ernest Tubb's idol was Jimmie Rodgers, the first popular Country and Western (C&W) recording artist. Tubb was so enthralled by Rogers that he purposely never heard or met Rogers in person for fear that Rogers ". . . would say or do something that would upset the image I had of him (p. 11)."

Even though the majority of show people reported the importance of seeing a master performer on their own careers, they did not indicate that these *masters* were role models for them. With few exceptions they did not attempt to act as a disciple of an older performer or follow in the footsteps of the master. One of the few who apprenticed himself to an older performer was the magician Howard Thurston. The process of building an act (described in a following chapter) usually entailed borrowing bits and pieces of others' acts while attempting to forge a distinctive persona and act.

Early psychic and financial rewards associated with entertaining. The successful performers, the ones who make it big, are able to connect with their audiences so that there is a *flow* in two directions across the footlights. As Gilbert Seldes (Toll 1982:31) said of Al Jolson "One has forgotten there still existed in the world a force so boundless, an exhilaration so high and that anyone could still storm heaven with laughter and cheers." Al Jolson said, "When you have a crowded house, you can feel the electric what-do-you-call-it surging across the footlights between your audience and yourself and you know you've got 'em (Toll 1982:9)."

This exchange of energy between performer and audience creates a psychic *high* which performers are ever-seeking to re-experience. Slightly over 65% experienced this *flow* early in their careers, a few on their very first public performance, e.g., Eddie Fisher, Melissa Etheridge, Travis Tritt, Ward Hall. As Fanny Brice said, "There's no thrill more wonderful than that which comes from that feel of a friendly audience, and it is a thrill that comes more than once in a lifetime (Stein 1984:273)." Rodney Dangerfield said the *love* exchanged between audience and performer is the peak experience for performers; it is the payoff for all the frustrations and disappointments. And, as will be discussed later, indifference or hostility from the audience are show peoples' greatest fears.

Together with the psychic reward for amusing an audience, performers discovered that "it pays." Churches often take up collections for gospel singers; so performers like Sam Cooke supplemented their families' incomes with gospel appearances. More performers earned money by performing on the street. This extra money contributed significantly to their families' income, and, as was often the case, freed them from less onerous duties like working on the farm.

Turning points. Seeing the ideal performer and experiencing the *flow* reinforce the novice's interest and dedication to show business. Yet, before a performer can safely quit her "day job" she must receive some reassurance that she has a future in show business. Turning points are events which lead to a change or reinforce occupational or career direction.

Getting the first big break. Because show business is such a high risk endeavor, "just so" stories about "the big break" abound. Some stories are clearly apocryphal; some are embellished in the telling, and all are recounted as examples of "how it can happen." The first big break is taken as an omen that one has chosen the right occupation.

The standard Hollywood musical, **Singing in the Rain,** has the young, talented, ingenue replacing the older star, always with predictable results . . . "next day on your dressing room they've hung a star." Typically, the early breaks included a) invited to "open" for a headliner; b) offered a recording contract with a small, independent label; c) act seen and favorably reviewed by a major star or agent. A compliment from a star or agent is an especially powerful incentive.
Jim Carrey came to the attention of Rodney Dangerfield who both encouraged the younger comic and recommended him to others.

Getting an agent. Almost half of the performers (47.1%) got their first show business job by actively seeking it. They went to agents, bookers, venues and radio stations seeking work; whereas, 13.7% got their first job through family connections, and 16.7% through friends. Only 15.7% were actually recruited by agents, bookers, promoters or managers. However, signing with an agent and/or manager was a major turning point in pushing fledgling show folks into committing to the show business path.

Most of the feature strippers (Boles 1974) I interviewed had managers, most often their husbands. The manager worked with agents in arranging bookings, negotiating contracts, writing publicity, and insuring that the environment in the clubs worked to the advantage of the client. When I met the legendary Sally Rand in 1970, she was her own manager and spent long hours on the phone daily calling agents and arranging bookings. In strip clubs features were the stars, and their managers ensured that the musicians could and would play their music and that none of the other dancers would duplicate their gimmick or outshine their performance.

Agents and/or managers (sometimes agents become managers) are primary recruiters and molders of talent. Good ones can spot talent and help a performer develop an act and a persona. For Harry Belafonte his introduction to Monte Kay, the jazz club owner and later his personal agent and manager, was key to his early success. Melissa Etheridge reported that her first manager said she was a reincarnation of Judy Garland, a compliment bound to give any fledgling performer a psychic boost.

Bruce Springsteen started performing when he was 15. In the New Jersey area there were 300+ bands for every job (p. 37); so Bruce was advised first by his parents and then by his band's manager to get a regular job. "He told me a dirty word. He told me to work (p.42)." However, Bruce was encouraged by John Hammond, the legendary talent scout whose discoveries include Billie Holiday and Bob Dylan. When Hammond first heard Springsteen, he said, "I reacted with a force maybe I'd felt three times in my life. I knew at once that he would last a generation (p. 59)."

Mariah Carey's career was advanced by Tommy Mottola, the then head of CBS Columbia. He designated her "priority artist" and gave her the full treatment including heavy promotion for her recordings and tours. She eventually married Mottola, but has since divorced.

Harry Houdini went from spectacular failure to spectacular failure; his beloved mother begged him to come home and become a locksmith. He finally decided that show business was not for him when Martin Beck, the head of the Orpheum circuit (the leading vaudeville circuit at the time) criticized his act and then hired him.

> And as for your act—it's terrible . . . But your act has no routine. . . There are two things I like. I'd like to see you working for me, just doing those two effects (p. 62).

The great comic, Fred Allen, began his show business career as a juggler and then started working jokes into his act. His first agent, Sol Cohen, is reported to have given him important advice, "Louder up you gotta talk."

Breaking the ties that bind. While certain events like finding an agent or getting noticed by important people push the novice toward entertainment, the concerns of family, friends and spouses as well as the difficulties and disappointments associated with the field direct the beginner toward rethinking a show business career. Even though most performers had their first taste of live performance as children, they held a variety of non-performing jobs before they finally committed to show business. Harry Belafonte served a stint in the navy, Oliver Hardy owned and operated a movie theater, John Phillips sold burial plots, Lenny Bruce was a farm hand and Mel Tillis a baker.

An important factor in nudging the novice toward making a commitment was lack of perceived alternatives. At some point the majority of the sample came to believe that they had no valid alternative to show business. Real or perceived rejection by family was a major consideration. Due to their work, e.g., stripping, working in bars, brothels and other unsavory venues, or their behavior (alcohol and/or drug abuse, promiscuity), they became estranged from home and family. Georgia Sothern, the burlesque stripper, said of her transformation from Hazel Anderson to Georgia Sothern, feature stripper:

> This can't be real. But it was real. Who would wake up if she could from the nightmare that was a kid named Hazel Anderson, but she's the one that's not real anymore. Little Hazel died back there in New York City when she was dumped broke and confused by that louse Gene when The Four Daisies act came to a close. There no longer was anyone I knew named Hazel Anderson. Georgia Sothern was born and was maturing (p. 40).

Some performers spent time in jail or various rehabilitation programs including Lefty Frizzell, Hank Williams, Etta James, Billie Holiday and Howard Thurston. Others who left before they graduated from high school acknowledged that their lack of education would hinder them in any other occupational pursuit. These show people dealt with conflict from family and kin in various ways. Tammy Wynette took her children with her when she moved to Nashville to try to break into country music while Loretta Lynn left hers at home with her husband. Some husbands like Mel Tillis left his wife at home while he toured; others divorced. Almost without exception, all made it clear to family, spouses, children and friends, that the pursuit of their careers came first. All through their careers, these entertainers continued to place career above any other consideration.

In sum, the vast majority of the sample's introduction to show business followed a somewhat similar path: early exposure to live performance, psychic and financial rewards associated with performance, and fortuitous events which encouraged the novice to giving "making a living in show business" a shot. This general scenario is consistent across generational and racial lines. However, the early experiences of female performers are somewhat at variance with that of the males. Only a relatively small minority of the females had the knock-about, on-the-street childhoods of the males. Typically, female performers like Doris Day, Dinah Shore, Ethel Merman, Barbara Cook, Trisha Yearwood, Barbara Mandrell, Reba McEntire, Judy Collins, Carol Lawrence, and Phyllis Newman came from stable homes and began their careers in "respectable" venues.

A few females spent their early years in less respectable venues: Janis Joplin, Etta James, Tina Turner, Tempest Storm, Billie Holiday. Janis Joplin sang on the streets, panhandled and sold speed and heroin. Performing in respectable clubs was more difficult for Black than White performers as, until recently, Blacks, unless they were stars, were relegated to the "chitlin circuit" where working conditions compared unfavorably with the old burlesque houses.

Further, a number of female performers were "protected" by males, usually fathers but sometimes boyfriends, agents, or husbands, e.g., Reba McEntire, Barbara Mandrell, Mariah Carey, Trisha Yearwood, Loretta Lynn, Jett Williams. These performers had men who could and would both physically protect them and stand between them and the many predatory agents, bookers, and hangers-on in the entertainment business.

While there is a common general path for the majority of the show people, there are significant differences in the early experiences of these performers. In the following chapter I identify three major career tracks with a view toward examining the relationship between career track and later career developments.

CHAPTER SIX

ANOTHER OPNIN': ANOTHER SHOW: BEGINNERS' CAREER TRACKS

The data presented in the previous chapter show that around 80% of the entertainers began their careers by the time they were 14. These performers discovered their talents early and proceeded, often by fits and starts, to develop their performing skills. However, not all the sample followed that pattern. In this chapter I analyze the three primary career tracks of the show folks as they begin their performing careers.

Born in a trunk. Thirty or 25.6% of the sample had either close kin in show business or family members who dedicated themselves to launching their children's performing careers. Twenty-five performers had one or more parents or close kin in show business or related fields. Three of those parents were not involved with their children during their formative years. Additionally, three had one parent who, though not a performer, pushed, prodded, cajoled, and sponsored the child into performing at an early age. Ten entertainers' parent(s) worked closely with them during their childhood. Most of the show people in this group first performed before live audiences and/or for money by the time they were ten.

Sammy Davis, Jr. Gunther Gebel-Williams, Prince, Jerry Lewis, Whitney Houston, Red Skelton, Georgia Sothern, and Phyllis Newman, among others, grew up in show business. Georgia Sothern started working with her uncle when she was four.

> He was always teaching me new dances and songs and comedy routines. Even then I was in love with show business. For me it was the only thing in the world that meant anything at all (p.9).

Jerry Lewis' and Phyllis Newman's parents were both full time performers and both began performing with their parents by age ten. Sammy Davis, Jr., became part of his father's and "uncle's" act when he was three.

> My home has always been show business. That's where I've lived since the age of three. I've slept in hotels and rooming houses, in cars, or trains and buses, in our dressing rooms, with my father and a man I called my uncle, Will Matin. . . But home was where the lights were, the people out front, the laughter and applause (pp. 1-2).

Other performers' kin provided knowledge and encouragement. Prince's father gave invaluable guidance as did Chico Marx's and Al Flosso's uncles. Whitney Houston's mother, Cissy, and her aunt, Dionne Warwick, guided and encouraged her career. Red Skelton's father, a circus clown, helped start his career. Skelton always referred to himself as a clown, and he created a clown character as a fundamental part of his act. Mariah Carey's mother was an opera singer who started Mariah's voice lessons at age four. Peter Frampton's father had been a ukelele player, and Peter discovered his father's instrument at around age four. However, his mother, who had given up her own aspirations to become an actress, was even more influential in Frampton's career as she always encouraged him to pursue his musical ambitions.

Some parents, though not performers, took active roles in their children's careers. With the encouragement of his father, Fred Astaire's mother provided dancing lessons for him and his sister. At the prodding of their dance teacher and Astaire's father, his mother took them to New York City where they began their professional careers. Minnie Marx and Sarah Berlinger (Berle) managed their boys' careers with unwavering dedication. Minnie Marx was determined that her five boys should develop an act. Leonard (Chico) was the oldest and his mother's favorite; he became the leader of the **Marx Brothers.**

Milton Berle won a talent contest at age five; his mother saw his success as an omen. She was desperate to find enough money to raise her family, and Milton became the way. Mama Berle took Milton to movie auditions, and he got a number of parts, providing the money the large family required. Mrs. Berle devoted the remainder of her life to nurturing Milton's career.

No father was ever more involved in his children's careers than Joe Jackson. Jackson senior had a brief stint with a band, **The Falcons,** but little success. His wife allowed the children to play his old guitar and sing. When Joe discovered his children's talents, he immediately began to devote himself to jump-starting their careers. Michael first performed at school at age five and won a talent contest when he was six. Joe believed the **Jackson Five** should go public, and he accompanied them to endless auditions. Joe Jackson says of his investment in his sons:

> You have to understand that I saw the great potential in my sons. So, yes, I did go overboard. I invested a lot of money in instruments, and that was money we did not have. My wife and I would have some heated arguments about this 'waste of money.' But I was the head of the household, and what I said was the final word. I overcame her opinion (p.14).

Of the 30 performers in this track, 15 were White and five were Black males; of the females seven were White, two were Black, and one was of mixed heritage. Seven were Jewish, and only one grew up in a holiness church. Only two are "relative unknowns." These data conform closely to characteristics of the sample as a whole with the exception of White females. They comprise 19.7% of the sample as a whole but 26% of those "born in a trunk."

From the biographies it is difficult to discern the nature or quality of the relationships between the entertainers and their families. In many cases the performers appear to have been genuinely grateful for the sponsorship of family members, e.g., Sammy Davis, Jr., Barbara Mandrell, Reba McEntire, Phyllis Newman, Georgia Sothern. In other cases the entertainers clearly had mixed feelings about the involvement of their families in their careers: Michael Jackson, Milton Berle, Gunther-Gebel Williams. A few parents were either hostile to or uninvolved in their children's aspirations. Al Jolson's and Liberace's fathers disapproved of their children's choices. Jett Williams began her singing career after she discovered she was Hank Williams' daughter; he had, however, been dead for a number of years. Snoop Dogg, Billie Holiday, and Eminem had little or no contact with their performing parents. However, those entertainers who had no close contact with their performing parents clearly saw themselves as having *inherited* their parents' skills and ambitions. Jett Williams felt destined to become a country singer once she discovered her parentage. Eminem's mother reminded him that his father, who had abandoned them when the boy was six months old, was a musician.

Involvement of the parent(s), the talent, the ability to earn money, and the attention often caused resentment on the part of the entertainer's siblings. Chico Marx's brothers resented his dominance over their lives. They felt coerced into performing. Groucho particularly resented Chico, and his anger increased in proportion to the extent that he had to "carry" the **Marx Brothers**. Early in the career of the **Jackson Five** the siblings began to resent Michael's ascendancy. The more attention he received, the greater the resentment.

Milton Berle was the only entertainer who spoke in some detail about the resentment that his siblings felt because his mother devoted so much of her time to his career. Siblings are, by and large, the "faces on the cutting room floor" in the biographies and *autobiographies* of performers.

Gotta Dance: Gotta Sing: Starting on their own. Sixty-three or 53.8% of the performers followed a career track typified by: early discovery of a performing talent; realization of the benefits associated with that talent; and increased commitment to entertainment as an occupational choice.

All but five of these entertainers had performed before the public by the time they were ten years old. The median age for receiving their first financial compensation for performing was 8.5. Many discovered their *talent* by age four or five. They learned they could sing, dance, mimic and clown at home, in churches or synagogues, or on the street. They seemed to *know* their destiny was show business.

Jimmie Rodgers apparently decided, very early and very definitely, that he wanted to be an entertainer-----one of those rare and select people who are called, almost by divine right or intervention, to rise in front of other, lesser humans and do things that dazzle, delight and ennoble their poor benighted fellows. . . He made his mind up and headed straight for the mark (p. 22).

Outside the home, school, religious institutions and the streets were the three key locations where the majority of the sample got their first significant taste of their own abilities and the myriad rewards of life in show business. Several performers began their careers in school: Richard Pryor, Art Hodes, Mel Tillis, Barbara Cook, Bud Freeman, Norma Miller. They found that they received special attention from teachers and fellow students. Eddie Fisher's first public performance was at a school Christmas/Chanukah celebration.

> There were three hundred people there; you sang and the whole place went crazy. 'Oh, let me touch him,' everybody said. 'He won first prize.' I loved to sing, and I knew I loved it. (p. 10).

Other performers had their first taste of show business in religious institutions: Jerry Lee Lewis, Darlene Love, Sam Cooke, Tammy Wynette. Playing the piano and singing in the choir were the impetus to many careers. Additionally, a number of performers got their first taste of show business by performing on street corners for tips. They sang, danced, played instruments and did magic tricks. They learned how to hold an audience and brought home extra money to boot.

Of the 63 performers in this track, 31 were White and 16 were Black males. Two were of mixed heritage. Of the females seven were White and six were Black and one was of mixed heritage. Seven were Jewish, and 15 came from holiness backgrounds. Seven are relative unknowns.

Many of the performers in this track had the approval and support of family members: Sam Cooke, Oliver Hardy, Houdini, Freddie Prinze, Duke Ellington, Tupac Shakur and Fanny Brice. Other family members were not so supportive. Some parents, like those of Will Rogers and Dinah Shore, felt that show business was a waste of their children's talents and a sure route to penury. Others were opposed to secular music or show business environments. Jimmie Durante's father disapproved of Jimmie's choice of music (ragtime) and show business which he associated with alcohol and vice. The parents who belonged to holiness denominations generally disapproved of their children's choices. Some parents appeared to be unconcerned or uninvolved with their children's choices. Richard Pryor's, Etta James' and Augustus Rapp's parent(s) were themselves involved in illegal enterprises and evidenced little concern for their children's future prospects. All in all neither parents nor siblings seemed to strongly encourage or discourage the aspirations of those in this track. Rather as young children these performers set upon a career track which offered the prospect of money and attention.

I Won't Dance: Drifting into Show Business. In contrast to the entertainers in the first two tracks, the remaining 24 performers were generally late in discovering the performing talent, evidenced little early interest in performing, and became performers out of necessity. The median age for their first public performance was 12, and the median age at which they first performed for money was 17. Twelve were White males and nine were White females. There was one Black female and two transgendered individuals. Six were relative unknowns.

Six performers were either in outdoor show business (carnivals, circuses or medicine shows), or strippers. They gravitated toward the less prestigious segment of show business because it is generally more accepting of aspirants who have little or no discernable talent or stage presence. Heidi Mattson and Tempest Storm started stripping because they needed a job. Hedy Jo Starr and Lady Chablis found working in carnival girls shows and drag shows accepting. As Hedy Jo said:

> I ran away with a carnival because I knew that they {carnival show folks} would accept me. If you can't make it in a carnival, you can't make it anywhere. Carnies will always take you in and make you part of the family (personal communication).

Some of the performers tried a number of different occupations before they finally "hit" on show business. David Brenner was a writer and Jim Morrison a poet. Sam Kinison tried a number of jobs including preacher before he finally concentrated on comedy. Trisha Yearwood worked in the music business in Nashville before she finally decided to make a serious effort to start a singing career. Janis Joplin continually vacillated between show business and attending business school in an effort to become a secretary. Loretta Lynn, the great country singer, evidenced little interest in show business as a young wife and mother. She credits her husband, Doolittle, who bought her a guitar when she was 24, as the impetus to her career.

> Now that's what I mean when I say my husband was responsible for my career. It wasn't my idea; he told me I could do it. I'd still be a housewife today if he didn't bring that guitar home and then encourage me to be a singer (p.103).

A number of these performers attained great success: Jim Morrison, Tempest Storm, Loretta Lynn, Janis Joplin, Howard Thurston; yet, the majority's careers did not last as long or shine as bright as fellow performers in the other two tracks. Consider the careers of Sam Kinison, Louie Anderson, and David Brenner as compared with Jack Benny, Bill Cosby, Richard Pryor or Lenny Bruce. Of the entertainers in this track those that are still viewed as major stars (within their own specialities) are Jim Morrison, Janis Joplin, Howard Thurston, Tempest Storm, and Loretta Lynn.

In sum, the vast majority of the show people in this sample were either born into families with show business experience, or they discovered their talent at a young age and developed it over the years. Those who drifted into show business are over-represented with the relative unknowns, and they tended to congregate in the least prestigious venues.

The following chapter focuses on learning how to entertain. Developing an act and a persona and learning the *business* of show business are key components of making a living as an entertainer.

CHAPTER SEVEN

MY BAG IS PACKED; I'VE GOT MY ACT:
LEARNING TO ENTERTAIN

We learn how to perform a particular job in three ways: formal training, on-the-job, and experiential. People in the professions and skilled trades learn through a formal training program like medical school. Also, we all learn while on the job, instructed by more experienced workers and mentors. However, it is usually through trial and error we gradually learn what works and what does not. Most show people have little or no formal training, and may or may not receive help from others in the business. Most rely on experiential "trial by fire"; they learn from failure as well as success.

Learning to entertain involves three major components: 1) developing an act; 2) developing a persona and 3) understanding the *business* of show business. In this chapter I describe the processes by which the men and women in the sample learned to entertain.

Developing an Act. A performer must have an act and know how to sell it to an audience. Both are essential. Most show folks start as amateurs, playing classrooms, churches, revivals, and various community organizations or busking on the street. For most the distinction between amateur and professional is blurred. For example, Sam Cooke sang in church, and he and his family would be given money from the collection.

Performers generally serve long apprenticeships, entertaining for money and for free while they gradually develop their acts and personas. Art Hodes, the jazz pianist, said of his early experience before an audience.

> At high school the kids discovered that I could play piano, and they enlisted me to play during breaks in classes. I was popular, sought after, and I liked it. I didn't know it then, but I was getting a workout. I was learning, getting relaxed playing for listeners and watchers, and improving right along (p. 10).

His teachers were so enthralled with his abilities that Jim Rose was allowed to take "independent studies" in high school as long as he agreed to give one performance in every class each semester.

Show people generally begin their careers by developing an act, e.g., juggling, singing, tap dancing, etc. An act involves much more than just singing a song or juggling three balls. It consists of an opening, a middle and a closing or finish. At the beginning of their careers most entertainers were like Houdini (as discussed in a previous chapter) who had tricks but no act. Putting together an act may take months or years. Building a new act is often such a horrendous undertaking that some performers resist doing it and "go stale."

Georgia Sothern recalled how she constructed her first act in burlesque.

> I watched those strippers work, watched everything they did. The way they walked, the studied way they removed their clothing that always looked so casual but never is. I planned how I would do it on Monday when my time came. . . An act, I was putting together an act (p. 32).

In contrast Joan Rivers developed her first comedy routine lying on her stomach.

> I lay on the floor on my stomach with a pad and pencil. Getting an act turned out to be very, very easy. All I had to do was twelve hours of TV watching. When anything seemed funny, I wrote it down (p. 117).

Show people, in contrast to electricians or sociologists, are largely self-taught. Only 29.4% of the sample had any formal training. Doris Day was one of the few singers who had singing lessons and coaching. As she said of her voice teacher, "If I had to name one person who had the greatest effect on the career that was in store for me, that person would be Grace Raine (p. 35)." Phyllis Newman started tap lessons at three, and her dance teacher got her an agent when she was twelve. Art Hodes studied the piano at Hull House.

Some of those who did have formal training disappointed their teachers and/ or parents. Jimmie Durante was a student of a classically trained teacher, but he snuck away to listen to Eight Fingers Rogers play ragtime.

Formal training, books and tapes, other performers and observation are the sources of information show people used in constructing their acts. Only 3.9% learned from a spouse, 42.2% from other performers, 33.3% from family members, and 17.6% from friends. In spite of those resources 76.5% created their acts primarily through trial and error.

Musicians and dancers are more apt to have formal training, and magicians are the most likely to use magic books, tapes and store-bought paraphernalia. In the past mail order houses carried a substantial inventory of how-to magic books and equipment which young people could order. Currently, magic tapes explaining how tricks are done and presented are available for every beginning prestidigitator.

Eddie Field's uncle was an amateur magician who showed the young Field a few simple tricks, but Field's interest in magic blossomed when he made his first trip to a real magic shop. The autobiography, **The Memoirs of Robert-Houdin, Ambassador, Author and Conjurer Written by Himself,** opened both the world of magic and the possibility of fame and fortune to young Ehrich Weiss, later known as Houdini. Bill Boley's interest in magic was piqued by the magician who played his school assembly. His school had one book, **Fun and Games,** which contained a few simple tricks. Boley soon mastered every one. He then began ordering tricks from the **Johnson Smith Catalog**. When he was ten, Al Flosso, The Coney Island Fakir, first saw a stage show staring Harry Broughton; it was then Flosso decided to become a magician. The very next day after seeing Broughton's show, Flosso went to a magic shop and purchased **The Wizard's Manual and Modern Coin Manipulation** When he was 16 and working in a dry goods store, Augustus Rapp bought a book on magic for ten cents. Intrigued, he found a book about magic at the public library. He then watched the stage magician, Alexander Herrmann, perform. Rapp decided that magic was his calling.

Friends, family members, co-workers and spouses were also influential in teaching novices. Tempest Storm learned the rudiments of stripping from the manager of a burlesque theater. Bud Freeman, the jazz saxophonist, became friends with the jazz great, Jimmy McPartland, and together with some others they formed a jazz band. Josh White, the guitarist and singer, apprenticed with a number of Black, blind blues singers, including Man Arnold and

Blind Lemon Jefferson. The singer, Eddie Cantor, was responsible for turning Jimmie Durante from a piano player to a comic. Eddie Cantor told him, "Everybody likes you. Get out on the floor and tell jokes." Durante responded, "Gee, Eddie, I couldn't do that. I'd be afraid they'd start laughing (p. 27)."

Performers who began their careers in staged and choreographed shows like **Gypsy** had the benefit of professional coaching. Unlike the novice nightclub singer, the Broadway singer or dancer is coached and cosseted. A number of show folks in this sample had Broadway experience, including W. C. Fields, Fanny Brice, Will Rogers, Ethel Merman, Barbara Cook, Al Jolson, Carol Lawrence and Phyllis Newman. Carol Lawrence said of her work with Jerome Robbins on **West Side Story:**

> Never have I worked with anyone more tyrannical than Jerome Robbins . . . We learned, very quickly, that he demanded more of us than we ever thought we could give—and that if we didn't meet those expectations, we were out (p. 42).

Almost all the entertainers admitted to learning through trial and error, but, for the comics, experience before a live audience is essential. No comic knows what will play before an audience until he tries it out. In order to succeed, a comic must be willing to fail. Joan Rivers remembered her early gigs doing comedy in strip clubs:

> I could only persist, take a risk, continue creeping on stage, very tentative, with a lot of 'so hello' and 'uhs', a lot of stammering and a air of apology and terrible Robert Orbin jokes to cover bombing. 'Don't laugh; it'll interrupt my rhythm' . . . I was told by those tough audiences that I was not funny, not talented, perhaps not even human (p. 165).

Perhaps the two entertainers who had the most difficult apprenticeship were the animal trainers, Gunther Gebel-Williams and Clyde Beatty. They started out by cleaning cages and gradually worked up to spending hours feeding, training and teaching wild animals.

I Gotta Be Me: Developing a Persona. If a performer wishes to emerge from the chorus and become a star, she must create a persona to which the audience responds. As Willie Nelson said:

> What I do for a living is get people to feel good. It's not a power that I feel I have in and of myself. It is a power that is exchanged between me and my audience. . . The main thing is to attract people. I do it. I always thought that's what a musician is supposed to do—try and draw a crowd to hear you play. I started out thinking I want to draw attention to myself, and it was inevitable that it happened because of the power of my creative imagination (p.3, 68).

As it is used today, the term *persona* derives from the ideas of Carl Jung about the difference between the "real" person and the public mask or persona. The persona is the mask which the entertainer presents to the audience; the closer the persona to the real person (if such exists), the easier it is to maintain. The creation and/or development of a persona may be the result of a lucky accident or a carefully constructed creation. Travis Tritt notes that most singers begin their careers as "sounds like"; to succeed the performer must develop a distinct style, a persona which differentiates him from all the competition.

George Burns was a small-time song and dance man until he teamed with Gracie Allen. At the beginning of their partnership their act was still song and dance until Gracie said something in the middle of a routine, and the audience laughed. Burns realized that the audience liked her and thought she was funny. From then until her retirement, Burns was the cigar-smoking straight man and Gracie the comic. From observing audiences Clyde Beatty realized that the typical audience was more responsive when he appeared to be fighting for his life. He framed his act around the perception of fear; he usually drank a beer prior to his performance so that he would sweat profusely. The sweat pouring down his face convinced the audience that he was in immediate danger.

The great ventriloquist, Edgar Bergen, exhibited a reticent, reserved, Scandinavian personality which failed to attract audiences. He created Charlie McCarthy who was everything Bergen was not: brash, bold, irreverent. The dramatic contrast between the personas of Bergen and Charlie McCarthy powered the act. Bergen was the perfect foil for Charlie.

Some performers' personas developed over time. Michael Jackson slowly separated himself from **The Jackson Five** and began creating his own separate and distinct persona, using both his music, dance routines, and costumes to establish himself. The young Frank Sinatra gradually evolved into the mature finger-snapping, swinger surrounded by the Rat Pack.

Building a persona is especially difficult for comics. Milton Berle was very conscious of his persona.

> Flippant, aggressive, a wise guy, a corner comedian, big city slicker with a put-down, an insult with venom, with bitterness, with smiles, without smiles, a smart-ass, sure. I know my image. Christ—I created it (p. 53).

Any performer's relationship with the audience is critical. That relationship may be intimate and is often confrontational. Successful performers must maintain control over the audience. All performers have, at one time or another experienced the loss of control over the audience. Flawed sound equipment, excessive noise coming from either back stage or the audience, disruptions caused by hecklers or any number of other unplanned and unforeseen circumstances can disrupt the all-important connection between performer and audience.

Comedians are especially prone to lose audience control. If once lost, it is difficult to regain. Stebbins (1990) describes the put-downs, microphone tricks, and verbal styles comics employ to establish and maintain audience control. One of the comics interviewed by Fisher and Fisher (1981:2) said, "If you're not in control, people won't pay attention. You have to show them you're the boss. If there happens to be a heckler in the audience, and you find you can't control him, the whole audience will turn into hecklers."

In her paper on burlesque comics Salutin (1970: 163) described what happens when a comic loses control.

> The only time a comic will acknowledge his professional failure to his audience is when he feels he has been defeated and he no longer wishes to continue the show as it stands. That is, he no longer wishes to continue in the role of burlesque comic, and he is calling it quits for the night. For example . . . the comic might say, 'you guys are a ship leaving a sinking rat.'

All the comics in the sample addressed the problems they experienced trying to maintain control over their audiences. At the beginning of their careers, they had not learned "all the tricks of the trade" so they frequently failed, but as they matured, they learned audience management. Novice failing comics often resort to insulting the audience, blaming it for their mistakes. The older and wiser comic has usually developed a number of fall-back strategies. If one story or line of gags doesn't work, the experienced comic can switch to another. A well-prepared comic usually had several sub-routines which can be pulled out in time of dire need.

The successful comic has several choices of persona styles. The easiest is to be likeable: Gracie Allen, Jerry Lewis, Red Skelton were likeable; each had very child-like aspects to their personas. Will Rogers was a trusted friend who would say things about people in power that we might wish to but wouldn't. Jack Benny made his persona the keystone of his act. He was the butt of the joke. When Bill Cosby started doing stand-up, he used racial humor. When he didn't tell jokes about racial issues, his audience either left the club or grew hostile. However, over time, he ceased doing racial humor and, instead, featured his monologues about Noah, his other characters and his children. With this change his audience expanded exponentially, and he developed a successful television show. Others' personas were more aggressive, but the audiences generally laughed at their bombast. W. C. Fields, Milton Berle and Jackie Gleason worked well in sketch routines where their high voltage personas were integrated into the characters they played. Their personas were honed by years on stage: vaudeville, burlesque, and revues, learning what the audience would accept and how hard they could push without rejection. Two of the **Marx Brothers'** stage names (Chico and Groucho) derived from their personal traits. Groucho was, indeed, grouchy, and Chico was obsessed with gambling and *chicks* (women). None of these comics, even Will Rogers, was out to change the world; they just wanted to amuse it.

A few comics, however, had another agenda. Lenny Bruce is the patron saint of comic as guerilla warrior. His stream-of-consciousness monologues contained an abundance of what was then considered foul and obscene language. His point was that language, including "dirty words" is harmless. "Tits and Ass", the title of one of his famous "bits," forcibly argued that point. Richard Pryor was called the "Black Lenny Bruce" because he attacked hypocrisy and dealt with drug and racial issues. Both Bruce and Pryor had ardent fans; they also alienated many. Sam Kinison and Louie Anderson also developed confrontational "in your face" personas.

Joan Rivers was one of the first successful female stand-up comics. She describes the process by which a comic develops an act and a persona.

> What makes a comedian finally jell? What must happen before a comic can hit? What creates a comedy act? I know the answer to that now. The act evolves out of yourself----but not intellectually. It gathers emotionally inside you in a strange way a by-product of struggle . . . until you gradually, gradually acquire technique and a stage identity, which is not you but has your passion, your hurts, your anger, your particular humor (217).

Her comic model? Lenny Bruce, of course. As she says,

> Personal truth means to me talking about your pain, which means stripping everything away, showing all of yourself, not some corner of your life okay for audiences to see. When you open yourself up . . . perhaps the audience will not be your friend (p.309).

Of course, musicians and singers also create personas. Both Willie Nelson and Waylon Jennings did not become major attractions until they labeled themselves "outlaws" and projected an anti-Nashville/establishment stance. Bruce Springsteen projected a working class persona which matched his music. His career faltered when he fired his **E Street Band,** married a model and began to assume a more middle-class persona. Recently, he has brought back his old band, divorced his wife and reestablished himself with his fans.

In contrast to most other country singers, Trisha Yearwood's persona has been crafted by others, particularly Garth Fundis, a record producer. As a girl Yearwood sang for family and friends but had not considered a show business career. While a student at Nashville's Belmont College, she majored in music business and took a job as a receptionist after graduation. She started doing record "demos" and soon quit her regular job.

Yearwood and Fundis spent several years looking for the right manager; they finally met Ken Kragen, who taught a course titled *The Stardom Strategy* at UCLA. Kragen managed a number of successful acts including **The Limelighters** and **The Smothers Brothers.** His credo for success is:

> One event in a client's life doesn't make much of a difference, but if a manager can get three or more events going in a short period of time he can establish momentum, propel a performer to, in Kragen- speak a new plateau of stardom (p. 69).

Al Teller asked Kragen to define Yearwood's image. Kragen's response was,

> "Trisha Yearwood should be seen as a great singer who also is the most stunningly beautiful woman in country music (p.71)."

> Kragen orchestrated Yearwood's makeover, directed her photo shoots, and saw that she received award nominations. Eventually, there were three key brokers in building Yearwood's career. Kragen would be the chief executive, Fundis the chief operating officer, and Harris (the booker) the head of distribution and sales (p.163).

While many performers changed their names during the course of their careers, a few created another persona with a distinct name and style. Prince, Eminem and Garth Brooks have adopted new names matching new personas. Changing one's name and persona, especially in mid-career is a dangerous strategy. Fans equate a performer's persona with his person, that is, Waylon Jennings, Loretta Lynn or W. C. Fields are, in real life, who they "play" on stage. Fans feel duped when they find that their favorite performer is otherwise than presented. Performers, particularly stars, tightly control public access to themselves so that their fans will be unable to compare the persona with the real thing.

Once established, the entertainer is protective of his persona because it is, after all, his bread and butter. The persona is what the performer sells. The market for entertainment is like any other market, a function of supply and demand. In the culture industry supply always outruns demand (Friedman 1990; Rosen 1981). While a few performers may aspire to only performing in the chorus, most aspire to stardom. The star is unique; there is only one Willie Nelson, Joan Rivers or Will Smith; no substitute will do. If a substitute will do, then that performer's star status is in dire straits. It is the entertainer's persona which commands star billing and large salaries. Thus, once a successful persona is established, the performer must guard it because show business is, after all, a business.

While most of the show folks in this sample created identifiable, unique personas, some did not. Their lack of persona hindered their careers. Jan Stebbins, the author of **Dennis Wilson: The Real Beach Boy,** argues that Dennis clearly epitomized the **Beach Boys** persona but was overshadowed by his brother, Brian. Consequently, Dennis was always in his brother's shadow and lacked the opportunity to develop a unique persona.

Darlene Love sang backup for a number of stars including **Bobby Darin, The**

Righteous Brothers, Nancy Sinatra, Marvin Gaye and Dionne Warwick. Her group, **The Blossoms,** sang backup on records produced by the legendary Phil Spector. Over her career she made a few records under her own name but has remained largely unknown. She explains her lack of success by quoting her brother:

> Dolly (Darlene) was always ready to step aside and let somebody else shine. She never minded being the vice president and letting somebody else be president. That's what might have kept her from peaking in her career to the extent she deserved (p. 213).

In show business, truly, "nice guys finish last." Darlene Love was identified as a backup singer by those in the business and unknown and unappreciated by audiences.

There's No Business Like: Show Business. The novice performer most often does not have an agent, manager or even a spouse to help find bookings and negotiate salaries. If she is going to survive, she must learn the business of show business and learn it quickly. Bill Cosby discussed the role of business in show business:

> But I've no great artistic ambition. What show business mainly means to me is cash. . . A lot of people in show business leave off the word business. (p. 44).

For all but the most successful, performing one's act is the easy part; finding work is the hard part. The late, great fan dancer, Sally Rand, is a case in point. When I met Ms. Rand she was in her early seventies and still working. My husband and I spent several days interviewing her in her hotel room. She constantly made phone calls to agents all over the United States and Canada seeking bookings. She mailed reams of flyers to agents and bookers. She called friends to see if they had heard of any openings.

When Travis Tritt started booking himself into country music clubs, he found that club owners lied and cheated. He taught himself to write contracts. He spent years as his own manager until he became well enough known to attract Ken Kragen and the William Morris Agency.

Entertainers who work regularly are embedded in a network of show business connections: agents, bookers, friends and acquaintances, as well as various trade publications. Carnivals and circuses recruit through **Amusement Business**. Jim Coston provides a home page which lists the addresses of cruise lines and bookers who handle the entertainment on these ships. The **Street Performers' Newsletter** informs those who perform in public spaces about forthcoming festivals, laws concerning performing in public spaces and others news useful to buskers.

Novices, as well as those who are not stars, must hustle most of their own work. Those whose careers spanned the twenties to the fifties were often responsible for getting their own bookings, especially if they were not well known. Jimmie Rodgers, Woody Guthrie, Bob Wills, Ernest Tubb: they all took their records to radio stations in hopes of getting air play, and they personally called club owners seeking bookings. Magicians like Augustus Rapp, Al Flosso, and Bill Boley had regular contacts with a variety of venues including schools which provided bookings. When Rex Dane and partner started their mind reading and spook show acts, we booked the theaters ourselves. Traveling from town to town we visited the manager of every movie theater within a given geographic area. Out of perhaps 25 presentations, we might get a booking with three or four theaters. Hedy Jo Starr booked her own girls show, and Ward Hall his own sideshow.

Currently, the entertainment business is increasingly formalized. Many venues will only hire through a booker. MacLeod (1993) describes the role of contractor in the New York club date scene. The contractor hires the sidepersons (musicians with no supervisory responsibility) for the band leader once an engagement has been booked. Individual disk jockeys have very little power to select records (payola has been a federal crime since 1960), and many comedy clubs and so-called Gentleman's Clubs (strip clubs) are owned by corporations, and hiring is done through a central office. However, the Internet allows entertainers to advertise and promote themselves. Using the Internet some performers have become their own agents.

Crucial to success in show business is selecting the right venue and/or selecting the correct material for a particular venue. Beginners often don't have a real act, let alone a persona. Agents are usually more interested in providing an act for a venue than helping a performer find a venue suitable for her act and persona. Consequently, performers are booked into the wrong type of venue. While none of the performers in this sample quit show business because they bombed, many quit temporarily or seriously considered quitting. Jack Benny, Fred Allen, Houdini, Jackie Gleason and Joan Rivers are examples of stars who failed dismally during the early days of their careers.

Neil Diamond's early stage performances were disasters.

> The truth was, Neil was just as terrible on stage in 1966 as he had been in 1960. As he {Neil Diamond} came off stage, they were half-booing, and half not paying attention to the poor guy, only because they were waiting for The Four Seasons.... somebody big (p.45).

Paying Their Dues. It is a show business cliché that a performer must "pay his dues" before he can expect success. All of those in this sample paid their dues, even those who appeared to be "overnight successes" like Ricky Martin who, in actuality, had been performing since age four. All the novice show people experienced the following;

a) alternate periods of employment and unemployment
b) audience rejection
c) discouragement from parents, spouses, friends and show business professionals
d) trial and error in the process of building an act(s)
e) bombing
f) endless touring

In spite of all of these problems the show people persisted. They put together acts, developed personas, learned how to negotiate with show business professionals, and developed confidence in their own abilities. While just starting out, many voiced concern about trying to make a career in show business; by the end of their apprenticeship, they felt secure in their occupational choice. They committed themselves to show business and thought of themselves as professional entertainers. Rarely, in the course of their careers, did they look back and wonder if they had made the right decision. The commitment of show people to their occupation is illustrated in this favorite show people story.

> A guy walks into a bar. He is dirty and smells terrible. Another guy at the bar says to him, 'I know it's none of my business, but, buddy, you smell really bad. Isn't there anything you can do about that?' The first guy says, 'I know I stink; I can't help it. It's my job.' The second man says, 'What kind of a job do you have?' The first man says, 'I clean out elephant poop in the circus.' 'Well,' says the other man, 'Why don't you get another job?' 'What, and quit show business.' the second man replies.

The next chapter details the process of building and sustaining a career in show business.

CHAPTER EIGHT
CURTAIN UP/ LIGHT THE LIGHTS:
SHOW BUSINESS CAREERS

This chapter focuses on the final three career stages: establishment, maintenance, and decline (Stebbins 1992). As was argued in the Introduction, reputation is the key to any culture worker finding employment. Faulkner and Anderson (1987:887) define a career in the culture industry as "a succession of temporary projects embodied in an identifiable line of . . . credits." The culture worker's employability and the amount of money he can demand is based on how well his latest projects fared: has his book sold, how many tickets did his latest tour sell? Monetary considerations are important in the fine arts; they are crucial in popular arts. In order to maintain or expand one's reputation, the entertainer must be visible, that is, she must be performing. If show folks are "at liberty" too long, they are forgotten. There is one primary strategy show people use to stay employed.

Anything You Can Do, I Can do Better: Flexibility. As that grand trouper, Fanny Brice (p. 3) said:

> Listen kid! I've done everything in the theater except marry a property man. I've been a soubrette in burlesque, and I've accompanied stereopticon slides. I doubled as an alligator. I've painted the house boards and I've sold tickets and I've been fired by George M. Cohan.

The grand strategy employed by entertainers to maintain their reputation and stay employed is flexibility. The performers in this sample were neither wedded to a particular performance skill or style, venue or even persona.

Rounding to the next whole number, 59% acted, 16% clowned, 35% told jokes, 22% danced, 10% performed magic, 2% modeled, 47% played a musical instrument, and 60% sang. The median number of entertainment specialities engaged in was four. Milton Berle did sketch and stand-up comedy, acted in films, sang and danced. Will Smith began his career as a rapper and then starred in a television comedy and now is a film actor. Even Clyde Beatty, who strongly self-identified as a wild animal trainer, appeared in several films.

Show people will perform anywhere: skating rinks, side show tents, subway stations, or on the courthouse steps. Fully, 82% worked in clubs, 27% in carnivals or other outdoor venues, 67% on stages(musical theater, vaudeville, burlesque), 63% in halls (performance rooms rented by organizations for private parties like Bar Mitzvahs), 62% in films, 68% on television, 76% in radio, and 32% on the street. The median number of different types of venues performed in was five.

In contrast to many other occupations, changes in the types of venues in which entertainers find employment do not follow a straight progression from least to most prestigious. Milton Berle was a child actor in silent films and later "graduated" to vaudeville and burlesque. The street is the least and films the most prestigious; however, show people will accept almost any booking anywhere any time.

Working in Venues

What follows are brief descriptions of the working conditions in the major types of venues in which show people find employment.

Show Business Out of Doors. Outdoor venues are less prestigious than indoor ones. As noted a substantial number in this sample began their careers busking on the street. Singing, dancing, doing magic, telling jokes; these show people attempted to amuse passers-by. Most of those who started as street performers like Al Jolson, Willie Nelson and Josh White, retired from street performing as they were able to get better dates. Though none in the sample continued as street performers, several thousand show folks perform regularly in a variety of outdoor locations: subway stations, street festivals, as well as heavily traveled urban shopping areas. Various associations like the **Street Artists' Guild** attempt to organize these itinerant performers and provide information for them about working conditions around the country.

Six entertainers in the sample (Ward Hall, Hedy Jo Starr, Clyde Beatty, Al Flosso, Howard Bone and Gunther Gebel-Williams) spent most of their careers in outdoor show business; yet both Beatty and Hall worked in films. Also many well-known acts including Reba McEntire, Waylon Jennings, Willie Nelson and Loretta Lynn, play fairs, rodeos, and other outdoor events.

Outdoor show business is hard work but a great environment for learning how to entertain. One such environment is the carnival sideshow: "I always said if you could survive one year doing a sideshow, you could survive anything" (Johnny Meah in **Freak Show**).

The sideshow is called a 10-in-1 because it consists of 10 (or more) acts housed under one tent. Sideshow acts are of two types: working acts and freaks. Working acts are typically sword swallowers, snake handlers, fire-eaters and the like. Freaks include giants, midgets, "half and halfs" and others with physical anomalies. One of Ward Hall's sideshows included the following acts (p. 57):

> Marie and Cliff King, midget couple; Johnny, Marilyn and Kathy Munroe, knife throwing; Emmett, turtle man; Red Rush, human blockhead; Patricia Zerm, sword swallower; Pete, doing iron tongue; Rita Reed, illusions; Doreen Reed, albino girl; Johanna Webb, mentalist, Milt Robbins, lecturer Albert Short, rubber man; Gladia Stump, frog woman; with Mrs. Reed, Mrs. Short and Harold Stump on tickets.

Usually a carnival moves on Sunday. Depending on how long the "jump" (the number of miles between dates), the show opens around noon on Monday or Tuesday and closes after midnight. The sideshow performers do their acts in rotation as the lecturer moves the audience from one stage to the next. Also, the acts are required to *bally,* that is, they do bits of their acts on the stage in front of the sideshow so as to attract a *tip* or crowd which is encouraged to buy tickets for the show.

The acts perform continuously from noon until the show closes; the show opens rain, shine, snow or sleet. As Ward Hall says,

> I'm performing fifteen minutes out of every hour. When I'm not up, I'm checking the tickets, fixing the props or helping the freaks. Would I do it again {spend career in sideshow}—in a heartbeat. I worked to stay even, to keep my tent, my banners, trucks and crew. You don't get rich or famous playing sideshows, but it's been a great life (personal communication).

Among outdoor show people the circus has more prestige than the carnival. Circus performers usually only do two shows a day and travel in better style. The old amusement parks where Al Flosso spent most of his career have morphed into **Disneyland, Universal Studios and Six Flags.** These parks use variety performers extensively, but will, on occasion, hire A-list acts for special events.

Circus acts, sideshows and, occasionally, street performers are reviewed in some magazines, particularly **Amusement Business.** Successful, money-making acts are favorably reviewed. Agents and bookers are always on the lookout for good acts, even those who start on a carnival midway.

Hedy Jo Starr, Ward Hall, Howard Bone, Clyde Beatty and Gunther Gebel-Williams all expressed satisfaction with the career choice. Al Flosso, however, gravitated toward magic and ended his career owning a magic shop.
The appeal of outdoor show business is difficult for outsiders to understand. Sally Rand (one of whose husbands owned a carnival) told this story:

> Two carnies are walking down a country road in the pouring rain. The carnival has folded, and they are walking to the next town. They're cold, wet, and bedraggled. They pass a house and look in the picture window. A father is sitting by the fire reading to his children. His wife sits by his side, smiling at him and the children. One carnie says to the other, 'Look at that poor bastard. I'll bet he wishes he was in show business like us.'

The Club Scene. The club scene is always highly varied and changes in response to the types of music in vogue and the demographics of the audiences. The most prestigious clubs have always paid top dollar for acts. Clubs in New York, Chicago, Los Angeles and Las Vegas represented the zenith while strip clubs, honky tonks and clubs on the "chitlin circuit" represented the nadir. Getting booked into top clubs were career breakthroughs for Frank Sinatra, Jerry Lewis, Sammy Davis, Jr., Neil Diamond, Edgar Bergen and others.

For blues and jazz musicians, dancers and singers, certain clubs were important in establishing their musical credentials. Bud Freeman, Billie Holiday, Art Hodes, B.B. King, Eubie Blake, Ralph Sutton, Duke Ellington, Nat Cole and Etta James all spent most of their careers playing in jazz and blues clubs. For musicians performing between the 1920s and the end of WWII, clubs were abundant and jobs relatively plentiful. Music critics from magazines like **Downbeat** reviewed their work. These performers were embedded in a dense network of fellow musicians, club owners, agents, critics and devotees who evaluated their abilities and performances. To be invited to play with Duke Ellington or Count Basie was a sign that you were among the very best.

These clubs faded in the 1950s. Some performers left the field; Jess Stacy took a job as a mail clerk with Max Factor. Others like Nat Cole abandoned the **Nat Cole Trio** and became Nat "King" Cole, crooner. Some like B.B. King continue to tour.

Beginning in the 1960s folk music grew in popularity, and a number of clubs and coffee houses sprouted around the country. These venues booked folk singers, and, occasionally, comics. Once again key venues were located in New York and California. While the godfather of folk was Woody Guthrie, John Phillips (**The Mamas and the Papas),** Joan Baez, Harry Belafonte, Janis Joplin, Judy Collins and Jim Morrison all had roots in the early folk scene. Folk fans demanded authenticity; they insisted that the folk performers be committed to humanistic, liberal or radical social causes. Woody Guthrie was sympathetic to the Communist party while Joan Baez and Judy Collins continue to remain active in liberal movements. Janis Joplin, John Phillips and Jim Morrison sank into a downward spiral of drug use. Belafonte began his career singing jazz and pop but was not satisfied with the music. His interest in folk grew when he became part owner of a restaurant in Greenwich Village. As his career in folk and calypso developed, he acted as an advocate for civil rights. Though folk music peaked in the 1970s, Joan Baez still tours.

Hank Williams Lefty Frizzell, Ernest Tubb, Waylon Jennings, Loretta Lynn, Patsy Cline, Willie Nelson and George Jones spent most of their careers playing country music clubs (otherwise known as juke joints or honky tonks). Most clubs are small and so is the paycheck. Stars play them on their way up and on their way down.

Traditionally, country music fans have demanded authenticity from their performers. Barbara Mandrell's anthem, **I Was Country When Country Wasn't Cool,** epitomizes the importance of appearing to be genuinely "country." The well-publicized lives of country artists reflect the themes in their music: alcohol and drug use, crime, unfaithful spouses, and prison. Only a few including Barbara Mandrell, Reba McEntire, Garth Brooks and Trisha Yearwood, have achieved stardom without a public history of dysfunction. Of course, some fans do not admit these four into the country music pantheon.

Generally, country music performers showcase their acts before agents and bookers at regularly scheduled events at clubs in Nashville and a few other cities. They greet their fans at Nashville's **Fanfare.** Record sales, bookings and the number of fans who stand in line to get their autographs are all important gauges of a performer's reputation.

Beginning in the 1950s American teens started listening to a new sound: rock and roll, or as the classical guitarist Pablo Casals, labeled it: "poison put to sound." Rock and roll offered a synthesis of White and Black country blues; so many of the early performers had either country or a blues background. Supported by influential disk jockeys like Alan Freed, rock and roll came to dominate radio. Bands formed and toured the countryside. Major stars emerged: Jerry Lee Lewis, Buddy Holly. Later, variations on rock and roll competed with the earlier versions as other performers sought the limelight: Bruce Springsteen, Michael Jackson, Peter Frampton, Sam Cooke, Janis Joplin, Jim Morrison, Prince, Tina Turner.

In the late 1970s rap/hip-hop began to emerge in the South Bronx. Key players in the development of this musical form were the disk jockeys like Grand Master Flash who pioneered the use of *scratching* which turned the turntable into a musical instrument. These disk jockeys would invite local rappers to perform a "rap" while the record was spinning. Centers for the creation of rap music sprouted in New York City and Los Angeles, and, more recently, Atlanta, Georgia and St. Louis, Missouri. Will Smith, Tupac Shakur, Snoop Dogg and Eminem were important rappers. Queen Latifah was the first important female rapper with her challenge lyric: "A woman can bear you, take you, break you/Now it's time to rhythm, can you relate to."

Clubs specializing in rock and roll or rap are ubiquitous throughout the country; however, increasingly clubs featuring live music host a variety of acts rather than specializing in one particular musical format. Musical styles are also blended so that a band might play country rock and blues during the same set. To survive, let alone prosper, a band must be both willing and able to perform a variety of musical styles from classic pop to rap. The contemporary musician must be, above all, flexible, that is, willing to play whatever style of music is required.

Comedy clubs go in and out of fashion. During the 1960s Lenny Bruce was active in New York, Chicago and California, particularly San Francisco. Later Bill Cosby, Richard Pryor, Freddie Prinze, David Brenner, Sam Kinison and Louie Anderson toured across the country and Canada. The improvisational club, **The Second City,** nurtured a number of comics including Gilda Radner and Joan Rivers. Jim Carrey began his career in Canadian clubs.

Television situation comedies have become major buyers of comic talent; consequently, there are a number of comedy conventions where comics preview their routines before television executives as well as comedy club bookers. A comic who scores at one of these conventions may be offered a television sitcom. Freddie Prinze, Will Smith and Bill Cosby starred in sitcoms using their comedic talents. Comedy is a fiercely competitive field as there are comparatively few venues available in comparison to those for singers and musicians.

Clubs featuring blatant sex acts are the nadir of the club scene. Lenny Bruce called them "toilets", and he as well as Tempest Storm, Lady Chablis and Heidi Mattson worked in strip clubs and drag shows.
Strip clubs have changed dramatically over the years. In the 1960s clubs used live musicians, and the strippers had elaborate costumes and an act. The better clubs employed an M.C. like Lenny Bruce or Joan Rivers to do a comedy routine as well as introduce the strippers. Tempest Storm was able to gain a national reputation through publicity stunts. With the right kind of publicity a stripper could produce and/or star in a stage production and make commercial films.

Since total nudity for female strippers became the norm, strip clubs no longer use live musicians or employ trained dancers with costumes and an act. Music is produced by a disk jockey, and several dancers are moving on stage at the same time. Money is made from *table dancers* where the performer removes all her clothing while moving to the music on top of a small table. Some clubs even allow *lap dances.* The opportunity for these performers to gain publicity is nil. Heidi Mattson was an exception. Since she was a student at Brown University, she billed herself as the **Ivy League Stripper**. She wrote a book and made several television appearances before her notoriety faded. Lady Chablis was featured in the best selling book, **Midnight in the Garden of Good and Evil** and played herself in the movie of the same name. She still performs at **Club On** in Savannah. Today there is a very limited opportunity for strippers or drag queens to improve their work situation, make significantly more money, or gain a national reputation.

In various cities around the world there have been a number of nightclubs or supper clubs with international reputations. Elaborate floor shows, dinner and dancing made for magical evening for patrons. Many of these clubs were located in central city hotels and were sustained by conventioneers. Frank Sinatra, Sammy Davis, Jr, Eddie Fisher, Carol Lawrence, Jackie Gleason, Edgar Bergen, Jack Benny and Red Skelton were frequent performers. Currently, there are very few of these venues remaining in the United States. Most American hotels have found them too expensive to maintain. The major exception is, of course, Las Vegas where the hotels support elaborate floor shows. Jack Benny, Liberace, Red Skelton, Frank Sinatra, Sammy Davis, Jr., Jr, and Edgar Bergen were regulars. Headlining in Las Vegas is the zenith of the nightclub business at present.

Currently, much of the music scene depends on recorded music. Urban clubs featuring combinations of rap, rock and other contemporary formats rely almost entirely on recorded music. The major stars like Tupac Shakur, Snoop Dogg, Queen Latifah, Eminem and Ricky Martin tour in stage productions as do the older stars like Springsteen. Still, thousands of small clubs featuring live music survive, if not thrive, in towns and cities across the country.

Stage Shows. These come in great variety. Burlesque and vaudeville theaters are stationary; the acts toured. Vaudeville had more prestige than burlesque, but often performers played both simultaneously. Milton Berle, Chico Marx, Red Skelton, Fanny Brice, Ann Sothern, Jackie Gleason, George Burns and Fred Allen are just a few of the show people who spent part of their careers in one or both of those venues. The careers of vaudeville and burlesque performers were closely followed. Those who pleased their audiences were hired for better circuits or Broadway stage shows. They were lured to California to appear in films and on radio.

Musical theater most often originates in New York. Ethel Merman, Al Jolson, W. C. Fields, Carol Lawrence, Barbara Cook and Judy Newman are all strongly identified with musical theater. Magicians like Harry Houdini, Bill Boley, Howard Thurston and Augustus Rapp toured in stage productions. Houdini and Thurston played large cities all over the world; whereas, Rapp and Boley brought their acts to small towns.

Touring with a major stage production is essential to the careers of musicians and singers. Tours are used to launch a new album or maintain name recognition. All the musical stars in this sample have either organized their own tours or been part of a major tour featuring several acts. Musicians and vocalists rarely make money from record sales as most recording companies deduct the costs of making and promoting records and videos from the performers' royalties. "Performers rarely see a penny of CD royalties . . . musicians typically must

sell a million copies for a CD to receive a royalty check (Mann 2000)."
Musicians make money from ticket sales and souvenirs.

Touring is emotionally demanding and physically exhausting; however,
for many, it is the highlight of their performing careers. Those who have
experienced the adulation of thousands of screaming fans find that experience
an emotional *high,* unlike any other experience.

A number of magazines closely follow the financial fortunes of tours: has the
tour sold out; how much money did the tour make; what did the reviewers
have to say? A performer's reputation can be severely damaged by a failed tour.
Occasionally, a star cancels in the middle of a tour, a reputation disaster.

Halls. Playing weddings, banquets, children's birthday parties, Bar Mitzvahs
and the like is a major source of employment for many small time entertainers
or those on their way up or down. Fees vary depending on the reputation of
the performer, the size of the audience and the amount of time the performer
is required to fill. A magician or a clown may charge as little as $50 for a
child's birthday party; while an A-list performer may make $50,000 for a
convention appearance.

Some small time performers advertise and promote themselves via cards,
word-of-mouth, and the Internet. Others work through agents and bookers.
Various Speakers Bureaus handle after-dinner and motivational speakers. In
convention cities bookers handle an entire entertainment package, providing
hostesses, entertainers, speakers and the like.

Staying Booked

The number one concern of all entertainers is staying booked. At some
stages in their careers many of the show people in this sample had more
bookings offered than they could accept. All had periods when they had few
or no bookings. Those at the peak of their careers could remember the time
when they couldn't find a job. Show people rarely take staying booked for
granted.

Excluding those who died prematurely (Freddie Prinze, Tupac Shakur, Gilda
Radner, Sam Kinison, Hank Williams, Buddy Holly, Jim Morrison, Patsy
Cline) and those who are early in their careers (Eminem, Ricky Martin) in
terms of income and reputation the entertainers generally peaked between
the ages of 35 and 45. Musicians tend to be somewhat younger and comics

somewhat older. Variety artists' careers don't peak like musicians and comics, but they can hold steady for a number of years. A magician or a vent with a good act can stay booked.

Most performers who become major stars only have a few short years there. As Garth Brooks said, "You only get a certain time; Elvis had seven good years. The Beatles had seven years before the breakup (Feiler 1999:13)." Still, few performers who can still walk or crawl on stage retire. Show folks perform till they drop. As Ernest Tubb (p. 292) said about retirement:

It's like anything else—you're either in or you're out. I've seen people try to slow down before, and after awhile they're out. I like what I do If you keep a band, they have to make a living. You have to work to live, and you have expenses to meet, like my bus. It costs me $100 a day to move my bus.

Key Career Maintenance Strategies. Show business careers are maintained through the judicious use of several key strategies.
Your Persona Working for You. If a performer establishes a persona which is popular with the public, she can use it in a variety of venues and formats. In commenting on his long and successful career, Jack Benny (p. 295) said:

In the first place to be real successful, your public must like you very much. They must have a feeling like, 'Gee, I like this fella—I wish he was a friend of mine.' If they like you, you may think sometimes that you are doing a bad show and you're not at all. But if they don't like you, you cannot do a good show.

Also, in discussing the power of his own persona, Benny (p. 295) said:

I can open with a couple of stingy jokes and everybody screams. Well, a lot of comedians who haven't got those characterizations have to make good as comedians, not as an institution—household words.

Benny was able to use his persona in his television series as well as appearances in Las Vegas. Dinah Shore, Doris Day, Mel Tillis, Red Skelton, Jackie Gleason, W. C. Fields and George Burns transferred their personas successfully to the mass media.

A few have attempted to change their personas, usually with disastrous results. Prince has changed names and lost listeners but has recently reemerged as

Prince and completed a successful tour. On the other hand in 1999 at the
height of his career Garth Brooks tried on a new persona, Chris Gaines-
rock musician. This new persona has not caught on with the fans. However,
sometimes a new persona is just what is needed. Richard Pryor was doing
straight stand-up for several years but was becoming increasingly dissatisfied
with his persona and act. His discontent finally erupted one night in the
middle of his act at the **Aladdin** in Las Vegas when he stopped and said,
"What the fuck am I doing here?" and walked off the stage. He spent the
next several years reworking his act and developing new characters including
his most popular **Mudbone.** The new Richard Pryor emerged with the now
famous video, **Richard Pryor—Live in Concert.** Rather than attempting a
new persona or act, most show people work hard at selling themselves and
their acts, honing the skills and seeking "the next big break."

Seeking the Next Big Break. Show folks and their agents and managers are
continuously looking for new opportunities. They read trade magazines like
Variety and scour the Internet. They correspond with friends, acquaintances
and people "in the business" about forthcoming tours, television series
and screen plays. Performers themselves often excel at recognizing when a
particular vehicle is right for them. Sinatra rejuvenated his flagging career by
fighting hard to play Maggio in **From Here to Eternity.**

Still, show folks mythologize "the next big break." For those who never
attained fame, the big break is always right around the corner. Successful
performers believe that a new opportunity will maintain momentum, and
those whose careers have peaked pray for a breakthrough which will reverse
their descent. One's career is really over when the realization that "it's not
going to happen" permeates the *unrealistic optimism* of most show people.

Agents, managers, friends, former colleagues are called in to help engineer
the needed break. Singers look for good songs, comics rehearse their new
routines in small clubs or at "open mikes." A performer may put together a
showcase, usually held at a club where, surrounded by supporters, the new act
is performed. Hopefully, critics will write glowing reviews, and agents and
bookers will start calling.

On the Road Again: Touring. Major stars like Nelson, Springsteen and
Eminem tour as do Hall, Rose and Boley. Touring is essential to maintaining
career momentum or revitalizing a fading one. The rigors of the road are
multiple, but are especially demanding for women and racial minorities.
Almost all the Black entertainers working prior to the 1960s complained

about segregation. Stars like Nat Cole, Duke Ellington and Billie Holiday were excluded from the best hotels and restaurants. Many Black performers like Ellington preferred to tour overseas because they received much better treatment there.

Black performers usually had White agents, managers and producers which opened them up to criticism from those believing that these entertainers should use Black agents exclusively. It is only with the dominance of hip/hop and rap that Black agents, managers and producers have become powerful enough to further the careers of their stars. Also, Black performers were sometimes criticized for "going White." "Once again Will {Will Smith} was being slammed by old foes in the hip/hop community for being a fake and a sellout (p.56)." Prince was one of the first Black artists to realize the potential of controlling his own material. Early in his career he founded his own studio, **Paisley Park.** He advertises, markets and promotes his recordings and personal appearances on his own web site.

Historically, women have found ample employment opportunities in show business; however, the *business* of show business has been dominated by men. Female entertainers have been guided or exploited by male agents, managers, directors and producers. Clive Davis, the legendary head of **Arista Records,** guided Whitney Houston, and for many years Ike Turner controlled Tina Turner's professional life. Trisha Yearwood is mentored by Garth Fundis and Ken Kragen as Mariah Carey was by Tommy Mottola. Darlene Love and her group, **The Blossoms,** were regulars in Phil Spector's studio.

Patsy Cline was one of the few female performers who insisted upon following her own "instincts" about how best to manage her career. Female performers who insist in making important career decisions find themselves labeled as "unfeminine." Often middle-aged female performers are viewed as "tough" and "difficult" because, through experience, they became less pliable and willing to be exploited by agents and managers.

Life on the road is hard for women. They risk sexual exploitation by troupe members, "roadies" or customers. Sustaining a modicum of privacy is difficult; cleanliness, skin and hair care and maintaining a wardrobe are doubly difficult when traveling in a bus or sleeping in cheap motels.

Increasingly, women are taking control of their careers (Boynton 1999). From stripper to rock musician to Broadway star, female entertainers, like their Black and Latino peers, have access to the material resources as well as the knowledge and self-confidence to direct their own destinies. Following the footsteps of the great Sally Rand, Queen Latifah, Melissa Etheridge, Reba McEntire are examples of women who have assumed control over the management of their careers.

Life on the road is hard. Milton Berle said:

> You want to know what a Jew's doing eating corned beef on white bread with mayonnaise, you go spend your childhood moving across the country eating in diners and hash houses and railroad lunch counters and dumps you can't even imagine, and you'll find out (p.8).

Willie Nelson (pp. 344-6) lists the "60 great lies on the road" which include:
1. The booking is definite.
2. My agent will take care of it.
16. Yes, the spotlight will be on you during your solo.
23. We'll have the flyers made tomorrow.
56. The tour itinerary you can count on to be correct.

Throughout their careers, the majority of this sample played one night stands and/or went on extended tours. No matter the rigors of the road, the stars as well as the lesser-knowns kept up a schedule of appearances as long as they could obtain bookings.

Managing the Audience. To keep working show people must please their audiences, not an easy task. Club performers and musicians find their audiences often ignore them. As discussed previously (Frederickson and Rooney 1988) the audience may define the entertainer as not present—*nonpersonhood*. Audience members may laugh, talk, walk around or even sleep during the performance.

Overt hostility often occurs. Strippers and drag queens are the recipients of verbal and physical assaults (Boles & Garbin 1974b). Comics are especially vulnerable to verbal assaults (Stebbins 1990; Fisher & Fisher 1981; Salutin 1974). Comics possess a repertoire of retorts to hurl at offenders. The more erudite may quote Voltaire: "My prayer to God is a very short one:' make my enemies ridiculous.' God has granted it." More pointed: "Red sails in the sunset; why don't you?", or "Ladies and germs," or, perhaps, "You're what happens when cousins mate." Show people in low status venues like sideshows, country music or strip clubs, deal with more open audience hostility than those on a Broadway stage or a Las Vegas showroom.

While it is tempting for the entertainer to outloud or insult an audience member, losing control of an audience damages the reputation of the performer. Show business media report when entertainers are booed. Sometimes the audience walks out, leaving the entertainer performing to an empty hall. Agents and bookers avoid hiring performers who develop a reputation for disputations with their audiences. Jim Morrison, Lenny Bruce, Sam Kinison, and Richard Pryor were known to have contentious audience relations which eventually made them difficult to book.

Bombing is a ghastly experience. The sound of silence curdles the blood; 42% of the sample reported fearing bombing, and an additional 22% were concerned about "fans who turn on you." While the novice show man may blame himself for bombing, the experienced performer almost invariably blames others. The equipment is either inappropriate or not there. The venue is wrong. The audience is too stupid, drunk or lazy to appreciate the act. Bill Cosby discussed bombing with Johnny Carson:

> Cosby: We {Cosby and Sammy Davis, Jr.} went to Broadway, and bombed. We had about seventeen people sitting there, man.
> Carson: How do you explain that?
> Cosby: "Well, it was Sammy's fault. He wasn't drawing at all. My people were there (p. 42).

When a star bombs, it is the manager or agent who is at fault. It is the star's road manager's job to see that everything goes smoothly: the accommodations are to the star's specifications; the venue is set up correctly; the house is sold out. Any failure represents serious dereliction of duty and must be dealt with harshly. Stars change agents and managers frequently. Managers say their basic job description is "not letting the star find out that there is anyone else in the world." Yet, occasionally, concerns about audience reaction can lead the performer to vent hostility on the audience rather than on the hapless manager. During a benefit for human rights, Pryor was booed by a largely gay audience; his response was, "You . . . can kiss my happy, rich Black ass."

Developing a sideline. During lean times some performers have entered entertainment-related fields which keep them connected to show business. Over their careers 24% owned and an additional 10% managed venues, 13%

acted as agents, 19% as promoters, while 26% produced. A small number ran viable businesses connected with show business including Reba McEntire, Mel Tillis and Michael Jackson. Increasingly, musicians have followed the example of Prince and started their own production companies.

Over half (60%) were writers, and many considered their writing more important than their performing. Willie Nelson, Woody Guthrie, Hank Williams, Fats Waller, Mel Tillis, Jim Morrison, Prince, Tupac Shakur and Duke Ellington were all composers who wrote some of the best music in their genres.

So Long, it's been good to know ya'; Decline. Voluntary retirement is almost unheard of among entertainers. Most continue to work as long as they can secure a booking. The veteran performer, Willie Nelson, was sidelined with carpal tunnel syndrome but after a short hiatus, he will be back: "I will not let my fans down." After his long time partner, Gracie Allen, retired, George Burns soldiered on doing a "singles" act. A number of performers died while on the road including Sam Kinison, Hank Williams, Edgar Bergen and Fats Waller. The performer and sideshow impresario, Ward Hall, recently announced his retirement but is still talking about framing a new show.

As a general rule for those performers who achieve national or even international recognition, seven years is about the maximum length of time they can stay at the top. There are several factors which precipitate their gradual (or occasionally steep) decline.

The Persona No Longer Sells. Fashions change and some types of personas become dead weights around a performer's ankles. The hipster became outdated and those performers like Lenny Bruce, Sammy Davis, Jr., and even Frank Sinatra, associated with it began to seem dated to a new generation. The star-spangled, rhinestone cowboy persona faded to be replaced by the more "authentic" appearing style associated with Waylon Jennings, Willie Nelson and George Jones. Younger acts like Travis Tritt have adopted this "down home" style.

Entertainment Styles and Venues Change. As noted various musical styles have prospered and then faded: jazz, folk, crooner. Comedy has gradually become less physical and more verbal. Show people strongly identified with certain passé styles have difficulty finding employment. Crooners like Rudy Vallee, Neil Diamond and Eddie Fisher couldn't sell records. Comics who specialized in physical material either were unable to get bookings or gradually adopted a more verbal style. As the Marx Brothers faded, Groucho emerged as a witty game show host. The popularity of Jim Carrey may usher in a return to physical comedy.

Changing public taste also leads to changes in venues. Currently, night clubs and clubs featuring male, female and transvestite performers have gradually faded. It is difficult for any of sex-related performers to develop a national or even regional reputation. Entertainers who are strongly identified with any type of venue that is dead or dying may suffer a severe career handicap. Traditional outdoor show business, i.e. carnivals, circuses, medicine shows, have declined in both number and popularity. Consequently, those performers who worked in those venues have suffered losses of income and reputation.

Sucker Sore. Carnies use that graphic expression for the outdoor show people who finally get sick of customers, i.e., suckers or marks. Even though the vast majority of entertainers in this sample actively wooed their audiences, musicians and singers may come to dread playing the same songs repeatedly; magicians tire of the same tricks. Audiences are often unreasonable and demanding.

Performers who are sucker sore cease to concentrate on pleasing their audiences. They refuse requests, arrive late, leave early and are surly on stage. A number of performers in the sample evidenced becoming sucker sore including Joan Rivers, Neil Diamond, Richard Pryor, Jim Morrison, and Tempest Storm. One of the key duties of the road manager is to isolate the sucker sore performer from close contact with the paying public. Michael Jackson's tours were micro-managed to keep him "safe" from his fans as were the tours headed by Springsteen, Pryor, Brooks, Frampton, Morrison, Cooke, and Prince.

The Greatest Sin: Undependability. .Old age or ill health is not, in and of itself, sufficient to derail a vibrant career. Many are still major attractions in their seventies, eighties and even nineties. However, once a performer becomes undependable, career options severely diminish. George Jones, Hank Williams, Whitney Houston, Dennis Wilson, Jim Morrison, Janis Joplin, among others, all had reputations as "no-shows" during some stages of their careers. Most often "no-shows" have alcohol or drug abuse problems, a subject dealt with in another chapter. A reputation as undependable is the sure end of a career. Sometimes the downward spiral cannot be stopped as in the cases of Jim Morrison and Hank Williams. George Jones, on the other hand, has quit drinking and revitalized his career.

Do Not Go Gently into that Goodnight. Almost without exception the show people in this sample fought against retirement. They kept touring, traveling by buses when they couldn't afford planes and cars when they couldn't afford buses. They constantly sought new opportunities: the next big break. Sometimes breaks come from unsuspected places, leading to a new lease on reputation. What follows are a few examples.

a) A performer's hit song may be covered by a younger artist or even used in a popular commercial. Neil Diamond has experienced a revival because one of his songs was used in a commercial. Nat Cole's record sales have increased as a result of a posthumous duet with his daughter, Natalie.

b) Revival tours and television programs may propel performers back into the limelight. Revival television events like the one describing a fictional folk reunion in the film, **A Mighty Wind** often lead to a spate of personal appearances for the featured performers.

c) Recognition by or partnering with a younger performer may revitalize a flagging career. Loretta Lynn's most successful album in years was the result of collaboration with a young artist/producer.

So, miracles do happen. A career is never over until the casket is lowered in the ground. For entertainers, their career is their most important concern; all other considerations are secondary. In the following chapter the personal and family life of the show people in this sample are reviewed. The sacrifices in terms of personal relations that entertainers and their families make to sustain their careers reflect the rigors and demands of life in the culture industry.

CHAPTER NINE

IF MY FRIENDS COULD SEE ME NOW: THE
PERSONAL LIVES OF SHOW PEOPLE

Occupation is an important determiner of life outcomes. Our probability of becoming mentally or physically ill, suicidal or deliriously happy is related to the occupation we pursue. Many entertainers lead very troubled lives; their divorces, drug and alcohol problems, bankruptcies, and assorted sex scandals are featured in tabloids as well as mainstream newspapers and magazines. In this chapter I examine the relationship between entertainers and their families and closest associates with a view toward demonstrating the connection between their personal lives and the rigors of a show business career.

Relations with Family Members and Associates

Show peoples' closest connections are with family members, agents and managers, and entourage members. Most of the biographies scarcely treated entertainers' relations with spouses and children; some discussed relations (usually problematic) with agents and managers, and none discussed feelings of the entertainer toward entourage members.

Love Me or Leave Me: Marriage. A slight preponderance of the sample (42.2%) were married only once, while 41.2% were married either twice or three times. Only 8.8% never married and 7.8% were married more than three times. These data do not suggest that show people are engaged in wholesale serial monogamy, but rather than their marital behavior patterns the larger society. A slight majority of the sample (53.9%) had between one and three children; whereas 28 (27.5%) had none, and 16 had more than three. B.B. King acknowledged 15 children by a number of women. In nine biographies no data on children were provided.

Because show people tour, work and play with physically attractive individuals, are pursued by fans and groupies in environments characterized by the presence of alcohol and illicit drugs, they are particularly vulnerable to temptations which make viable marriages and committed parenting difficult. The problems that performers have with marital partners are often related to whether or not their spouses are in show business and/or involved in the entertainer's career.

We Could Have Danced All Night: Careers in Sync. Some of the most successful marriages are between entertainers who either perform together or support each other's careers in specific ways. Some couples performed as a team: George Burns and Gracie Allen, Jack Benny and Mary Livingston, Fred Allen and Portland Hoffa, Jim and Bebe Rose, and Augustus and Mabel Rapp. While the wives of George, Jack, Fred, and Augustus were in show business before meeting their husbands, Bebe Rose, The Circus Queen, had no show business experience prior to joining the **Rose Sideshow.** Now her act includes lying on a bed of nails. Bess Houdini was part of a song and dance act until she met and married Harry. From then on she worked with him, often as his "silent" but essential partner in carrying out his miraculous escapes. Waylon Jennings and his wife, Jesse Colter, sometimes toured together, but he was always the star and major attraction. George Jones, and his one-time wife, Tammy Wynette, toured together but were not seen as a team. Each had his/her own fan base. Gunther Gebel-Williams' wife performed with him in the circus.

In the marriages mentioned above, with the exception of Tammy Wynette, the husbands were more committed to show business than their wives. These marriages appear to have been quite successful; the husbands maintained career momentum and made most of the career decisions. The major source of friction concerned the wives' desire to work less.

The majority of these team marriages occurred in T1. These couples started in vaudeville so they had the opportunity to see each other work before becoming partners. Once partnered, they honed their acts before hitting "the big time."

You're Mickey Mouse: Competing Careers. Sometimes two entertainers who are equally vested in their careers marry, a chancy arrangement: Carol

Lawrence, the musical star was married to the singer, Robert Goulet. During their marriage they usually toured separately. Though their relationship was strained, they managed to stay together until Lawrence had an abortion against Goulet's strong objections.

> We (Lawrence and Goulet) would be on the road for a long time. I also landed a Bob Hope TV special to promote my new nightclub act. I couldn't do those things if I was pregnant. Yet, I had put my career aside before, so why was this time different? (p. 154).

Competing career commitments is one problem; envy is another. Entertainers' popularity ebbs and flows; one partner may peak in popularity while the other fades. Those performers whose spouses competed (or appeared to compete) with them include Tina Turner, Eddie Fisher, Al Jolson, Tammy Wynette, Whitney Houston and George Jones. Ike Turner, for example, saw himself as the star and also the creative force in the act; whereas, others viewed Tina as the major talent. He was, as is well known, a physically abusive husband. George Jones was a major country star when he married Tammy Wynette. Though she never surpassed him with hard-core country fans, there was a period when her records like **Stand By Your Man** topped the charts. During that time Jones and Wynette appeared together on the **WPLO Shower of Stars.** While introducing George, Tammy said, "I've got six kids including George." They were eventually divorced.

Georgia Sothern married a burlesque straight man who attempted to take over her career. She said of him:

> . . . in his own way he was jealous of my success. I knew too that he would do anything to have me because in that way part of the success would be rubbing off on him (124).

In the 1950s Dinah Shore's career in television roared into high gear while her husband's (the actor, George Montgomery) floundered. "Dinah was on the ship that was headed to the moon, while George was on a ship that was capsizing and in danger of sinking (p.138)." He developed a television western, **Cimarron City,** but it bombed. He then produced, directed and starred in two films that opened to mediocre reviews. He and Shore eventually divorced.

Milton Berle married the performer, Joyce Mathews, twice. Though their work schedule frequently conflicted, that may not have been the major source of their marital difficulties. She was temperamental, and given to the grand gesture. She evidently resented Berle's success. She attempted suicide twice, once while married to Berle and while living with the impresario, Billy Rose.

At the height of his career, Al Jolson married Ruby Keeler, the musical star. When they went to Hollywood, Keeler's career flourished while Jolson's declined. Again, predictably, divorce ensued.

Occasionally, however, one performer will criticize the spouse for lack of interest in his/her own career. Tempest Storm's second husband was a singer with Duke Ellington's band, but he took little interest in his own career and resented Storm's attempts to help him. He discouraged her from trying to start a music career by saying, "One singer in the family is enough."

We're in the Money: Business Partners. Frequently, spouses are drafted into working with/for entertainers as road or business managers, press agent, promoter or general "flunkie." Sometimes these business relations turn out well; often they do not. As entertainers are prone to blame their managers when things go wrong, they are even more prone to blame the spouse. Female performers are more likely to draft their spouses into important roles than their male counterparts. However, male performers have delegated important responsibilities to their wives. Hank Williams' first wife, Audrey, was a strong woman who guided Hank's early career. Nat Cole's second wife, Maria, was largely responsible for changing Cole's switch from jazz to popular music. She controlled his career, even ordering his entourage to forbid any woman, even a family member, from entering his dressing room.

A number of female performers had spouses who played active roles in their careers, including Jett Williams, Reba McEntire, Phyllis Newman, Patsy Cline, Whitney Houston, Tina Turner and Doris Day. Sometimes these relationships worked out; often they did not. Doris Day's third husband, Marty Melcher, was her agent/manager. He alienated producers, directors and co-stars as well as forcing her into projects that she had originally rejected. Eventually, he became her producer and led her into financial and critical disasters. He also forced producers who wanted Day to pay him money before he would allow her to sign with them. As James Garner, one of her co-stars said, "I never knew anyone who liked Melcher (p. 257)."

We Could Make Believe: Marriage to Non-performers. The majority of those in the sample married people who were not connected to show business.

Some of these relationships evidently turned out well. The performer returned to hearth and home to rejuvenate. Home was an oasis of calm and safety, a "haven in a heartless world." Loretta Lynn's husband, Doolittle, evidently was satisfied staying at home and supervising the children. He provided Lynn with a sanctuary to which she could repair at the end of tours. Bill Cosby's relations with his wife, Camille, were, by all accounts, especially close.

> My life {Bill Cosby'} is a very, very happy one. It's a happiness of being completely connected, one of knowing there is someone I can trust completely, and that the one I trust is the one I love. I also know that the one she loves is the one that she can trust.
> (p. 47)

For some years Frank Sinatra and his wife, Nancy, seemed to have a reasonably successful marriage. Jackie Gleason's marriage to his second wife, a professional dancer and sister of the head of **June Taylor Dancers,** was reportedly happy. Art Hodes' wife stayed home and raised their three children. Both he and Clyde Beatty provided almost no information about their wives or children. Neil Diamond's first wife was a school teacher and supported him while he tried to sell his songs. His second wife was a homemaker and mother. Both of Jimmie Rogers' wives supported him while he tried to jump start his career. Evidently, Sam Kinison's marriage was very painful because after their divorce, his ex-wife was the butt of many of his comic monologues. After marriage, Edgar Bergen's wife retired from a career in modeling to become a full time wife and mother. As their daughter, Candice, discovered Mrs. Bergen felt that in the process of first supporting Edgar's and then Candice's careers, she lost her own identity. Probably the spouses of other entertainers felt similarly, but the biographies were not told from the perspectives of either spouses or children.

Some spouses were strongly incompatible. Though he never divorced, W. C. Fields lived with his mistress for years and was with her when he died. However, he largely disinherited her.

A performer may marry so as to improve his/her image. Sammy Davis, Jr, was criticized in the Black press for dating White women and was threatened by physical violence for dating the girl friend of a mobster. Davis said of his marriage proposal to Loray, a Black woman:

> This is a natural. Just what I need. A nice girl to come home to; someone I'll be proud to introduce as my wife; I'll come across with the public as Charlie Straight. They'll drop the 'wild kid' jazz in the papers. And the Negro press will go out of their minds; they'll eat it up like a hundred yards of chitlins. They'll be hugging and kissing, and front pages with come-home-son-all-is-forgiven. And Henry Cohen would be solved. One great move would solve all my problems (p.98).

Temptations of the road are many. Both male and female performers report numerous sexual encounters. During her lengthy career Tempest Storm claimed affairs with, Elvis Presley, Sammy Davis, Jr., Nat Cole, Mickey Rooney, Hugh O'Brien, Trini Lopez and Englebert Humperdink. Many of these men were married at the time as was Storm.

Mel Tillis, the country song writer and singer, had a stay-at-home wife and five children. As he says about the temptations of the road:

> It just isn't natural to be apart 200 or 250 days a year. That puts a strain on any relationship. It's even harder on children who only get to see their fathers when they come home from the road for three or four days . . . A traveling musician's wife carries a double load (p. 152).

Additional sources of discontent include money. During periods in their careers many performers do not make enough money to support their families so their spouses are forced to live hand-to-mouth. Both Woody Guthrie's and Jimmie Rodgers' wives were left for long periods with little or no financial support. Without the financial support of their families, they and their children would have starved.

Many of those in the sample made fortunes which can lead to dissatisfactions and unhappiness. Some spouses and/or kin complained that the entertainers spent too much money on themselves and their entourages. Buying food, drinks, and companionship for a bunch of "roadies" is expensive. During the height of his career Sammy Davis, Jr. carried thirteen people and 6,500 pounds of equipment and personal effects on tour; however, Michael Jackson toured with a crew of 150 and 100,000 pounds of equipment. Jackie Gleason often transported fifty or more members of his entourage in grand style across country. Providing hotel rooms, food, entertainment, drugs and/or alcohol and other expenditures for an entourage is exorbitantly expensive. Spouses may complain, usually to no avail.

Often performers feel, justifiably or not, that they are taken advantage of by greedy, grasping and lazy spouses and kin. The performer may be supporting an extended family. As Sally Rand said:

> Right now {1972} I am the sole support of seven people. You wonder why I am always on the phone calling agents, hustling bookings. Well, that's why. I've got all these people depended on me (Personal communication).

Fats Waller was continuously harassed by his ex-wife for failure to pay alimony and was frequently jailed. His friends, band leaders with whom he performed, and managers bailed him out so he could work. Before his untimely death, Tupac Shakur supported approximately 20 people including his mother, sister and her baby, and his aunt and her family. Richard Pryor and Louie Anderson also were expected to contribute money to various family members. In fact, most of the financially successful performers reported that they were viewed as "bankers of first resort" by kin as well as childhood friends. Some, like Jackie Gleason, were easy "touches" while others delegated employees with the responsibility of filtering requests for money.

Mama Mia: Children. As Mel Tillis remarked, entertainers and children are not always a good match. Most biographies mention children sparingly if at all. In the early stages of their careers entertainers' children are often left at home with grandparents or other family members while their parent(s) toured. If the parents became successful, then nannies were hired. Occasionally, the child was trotted out in front of the audience as if to show, "Hey, I'm a good mom/dad." This may backfire; at the beginning of a Las Vegas opening, Neil Diamond's son yelled out, "Please dad, don't sing. (p 180)."

While performers testified to loving their children, they rarely expressed more than perfunctory regret for spending so little time with them. Also, the children often had difficulty coping with the fame of their parents. Dinah Shore's young daughter yelled to some of Shore's fans, "Go away! She's not Dinah Shore today; she's my mother (p.158)." Sammy Davis, Jr.'s second wife pressured him to do more with his family. He reports on a time when his wife asked him to postpone a European tour to attend his daughter's birthday party:

> Darling. The one-man show at the Prince of Wales is very important, plus it's worth a lot of money. . . And, secondly, I can't dump on the Queen of England with, 'Sorry, your Majesty, my daughter's having a birthday Party'. . . Lie to her. Tell her I'm there. Tell her I'm hiding, playing spooky games with her. (p. 137)

When Jim Morrison's wife informed him she was pregnant, he said:

> If you have that baby, it'll ruin our friendship. A baby isn't going to change my life at all, but it would alter yours tremendously, forever. I—no difference. I won't support a kid. Any kid. I can't afford it, and I don't want the responsibility. (pp307-8)

Freddie Prinze married a young woman he was dating because she got pregnant. He and his wife started having marital problems soon after the baby was born. "She is not ready to be a parent and neither am I. I bury myself in prepping for my first film. I study again (p. 224)."

At one point in his career at the urging of his wife, Howard Bone left the sideshow and took a job as a night clerk in a hotel. Eventually, he abandoned his wife and child and went back to the sideshow.

Some performers do have positive relations with their children. The quality of the relations was, in large part, a reflection of the work environment of the parents. Circus and carnival performers tend to marry others in outdoor show business and raise their children in the business. Gunther Gebel-Williams' wife and daughter performed in the circus, and his son began working with his father when he was four. Frank Jr. and Tina Sinatra occasionally worked with their father, and Frank Jr. acted as his father's conductor on Frank Sr.'s last tours. Joan Rivers included her daughter in a television film about Rivers' life with her husband.

A few of the sample's children went into show business full time: Nat Cole, Eddie Fisher, Edgar Bergen, Frank Sinatra, Hank Williams, Woody Guthrie, Freddie Prinze, Jerry Lewis, Waylon Jennings, Mel Tillis, and Bill Boley. Often the entertainers were not helpful in furthering the careers of their children, and none of the children approached the success of their parents.

Relations between the children and their famous parents are fraught with a variety of emotions including, love, anger, resentment, awe and envy. Candice

Bergen's biography of her father is the only one in the sample written by the child of the entertainer; consequently, it provides a special insight into the lives of children of famous stars. Candice portrayed her father as a shy, undemonstrative man who expressed himself through his dummy, Charlie McCarthy, ". . . the companion with whom he would spend the rest of his life (p. 21)." Candice's mother, a former model, was a full time homemaker and mother. The Bergen family lived in a house in Bel Air. Her parents' friends were the Hollywood establishment, e.g., Milland, Minnelli, Stewart, Rubenstein, Reagen. The children of the establishment were treated like royalty: petted, protected, and privileged. Bergen (p. 57) describes a birthday party for six year old Lisa Minnelli (Judy Garland's daughter):

> The Gershwin lawn rolled on forever, and in the center, children spun slowly on a many-colored carousel, while others clustered around the Magic Lady-a woman in a long blue gown sprinkled with stars who pulled doves from her sleeves and rabbits from hats. There were hotdog stands and ice cream cones and clouds of cotton candy. Clowns clowned and jugglers juggled and sleek, shining ponies circled the lawn in a tiny, clipped canter for any child who wanted to ride. It was a fairy tale gift for a daughter born from a father who was a master of making fairy tales come true.

Bergen had a nanny, attended private schools, and, in addition, debuted on the **Edgar Bergen Show** at age six. As a child, she idolized her father, but as she grew older, they became estranged. Her film career began to blossom just as her father's was in eclipse.

> In spite of cockeyed erratic choices, my career was in the ascendance while my father's was in sharp decline. . . It was hard on him to see his fame waning He never actually complained about it, but it made me more uncomfortable about mine (p. 202).

Candice also began to experience resentment from her mother:

> My success had a double edge for my mother as well. Long known as 'Edgar Bergen's wife,' she had serious doubts that she alone had ever existed on her own. When I perceived the depth of her resentment I was hurt by it. (pp.202-203)

Tragedy, too, has struck some. Bill Boley's daughter was killed in an automobile accident. Bill Cosby's son was murdered. Sam Cooke's daughter drowned in a swimming pool which seems to have been deterministic in leading to Cooke's divorce.

In sum, most of the biographies mentioned their subjects' relationships with their children sparingly. Almost without exception career came before parental responsibilities. Evidence suggests that many in the sample resented the emotional and financial demands made by children, and, conversely, children resented parental neglect.

I Can See Clearly Now: Kin and Associates. A few of the show people performed with family members during some phase of their careers: Michael Jackson, Dennis Wilson, Willie Nelson, Liberace, and Chico Marx. Nelson's relations with his sister, who plays in his band, and Liberace's with his brother, George, were evidently smooth. On the other hand, Dennis Wilson resented the greater renown of his brother, Brian. As his fame began to outstrip that of his brothers and sister, Michael Jackson increasingly resented having to support his siblings. For example, when he arranged tours, he would plan first class accommodations for himself and second class for his siblings. With the support of his mother, Chico Marx was the titular head of the **Marx Brothers.** His mother forced his brothers to work with him and support his compulsive gambling and womanizing. Chico came to resent his more talented brother, Groucho, especially as Groucho made no secret of his passionate dislike for Chico. Finally, Groucho left the family act, leaving Chico resentful and angry.

As previously noted, entertainers frequently blame their agents and managers for career disappointments, on-the-road mishaps and the like. Slightly over 85% of those in the sample fired their long time agents and/or managers; 52% fired at least two or more agents during the course of their careers. Even though an agent or manager was instrumental in jump-starting a career, entertainers showed little loyalty. When one's career started to take off, it was often deemed necessary to move on to a more powerful agent. Sometimes agents or managers took advantage of entertainers by cheating them financially. Michael Jackson, Doris Day, and Red Skelton all reported having been swindled by people in their employ.

The relationships that entertainers have with those closest to them, i.e., spouses, siblings, parents, children and agents are difficult to sustain. Culture workers in general and live performers in particular are hindered in establishing successful personal relations by the following factors:

a) Because they tour performers are physically separated from spouses and children for long periods of time.

b) Entertainers work in environments which are not conducive to nurturing long-term stable relationships.

c) In order to build a reputation that will enable the performer to continue to find employment, energy must be devoted to one's career. The employed entertainer is one who has put his/her career ahead of any other consideration.

d) Finally, the entertainer is subject to the whims, prejudices, and tastes of the notably fickle public. You are only as good as your last show. Stage fright, the body's physiological and psychological responses to the fear of not winning audience approval, can dominate performers' lives and their relations with others. Entertainers *want and need* to perform before live audiences; conversely, they *fear* doing so. Their world revolves around seeking work, maintaining employability, and fear of failure.

In the following chapter the focus is on the satisfactions and dissatisfaction of work in show business. As previously stated, show people rarely retire: what are the rewards that keep them in the business? What are the costs?

CHAPTER TEN

THE OLD RAZZLE-DAZZLE: SATISFACTIONS
AND DISSATISFACTIONS WITH A
SHOW BUSINESS CAREER

As discussed in this book, the culture industry in general and show business in particular, is fraught with anxiety, disappointment and often heartache; yet, it continues to attract more people than it can absorb. Those in this sample remained committed to show business throughout their entire careers. In reading the biographies words and phrases which indicated pleasure or displeasure with show business were identified: "I loved meeting famous people;" "Seeing my name in lights was the greatest high"; or, "Not another tour; I don't know if I can do it." I also noted statements which indicated their greatest and worst show business experiences. Further, I sought comments which justified entertainment as a legitimate and worthwhile occupation.

Through examination of these types of comments it became clear that the show peoples' satisfactions and dissatisfactions were related to their orientation to their work. As a general rule all show business professionals wish to maintain a positive reputation so that they can continue to work. However, their orientations toward entertainment, its function and purpose, as well as their view of their act(s) determined what satisfactions they experienced during their careers. First, I will briefly review the satisfactions and dissatisfaction as voiced by the sample as a whole before discussing differences among those in the three work orientations

Bright Lights, White Lights: Entertainer Orientations. For the sample as a whole, 52 show folks indicated that entertainment has a positive function; of those, the majority (32%) believed that entertainment helps people cope with reality. As one said, "We bring sunshine into otherwise drab lives." However, twelve believed that entertainment could and should do more. Tupac Shakur felt that his raps assisted young African American males understand racial oppression. The goals of the remaining eleven are discussed in a forthcoming section.

Almost 55% of the sample mentioned money as one of the sources of satisfaction with show business while 23% suggested that travel was an important benefit. For many of those travel was associated with a sense of freedom and independence. This was most often mentioned by those in outdoor show business and country and western performers, their anthem: **On the Road Again.** As Waylon Jennings said:

> I used to love going to the carnival when I was little, especially to see the carousel horses. . . They were all wild, they were all free, they were all running. Not controlled by anyone or anything. That was what I was drawn to. The notion of freedom. (p. 40)

Additionally, those Black performers whose careers peaked prior to the 1960s testified that show business allowed them to travel not only out of the South but in foreign countries that did not exhibit the prejudice found in the United States. Successful stars like Duke Ellington preferred to work overseas.

Only 21% included meeting people as a benefit; those who did were usually referring to other show people. George Burns, Jerry Lewis and Sammy Davis, Jr. adored the company of other show folks. Also, some country stars noted their preference for socializing with other country performers. Twenty-nine percent saw entertainment as an adventure, and 34% thought it was glamorous. For those who came from poor families the lifestyles of stars were viewed as impossibly magical. Locations where celebrities gathered became the *great other place* (Schickel 1985) where magic becomes reality. Joan Rivers imagined that great other place:

> We . . . glimpse the secret garden of show business, the haven we think will heal our lives. . . Within those walls I would no longer be a wimp. . . I would become truly beautiful, bathed in glamour and adoration by my fans. . . When the telephone rang, it would be Laurence Olivier on the line (p. 23).

The dissatisfactions associated with show business include rejection from agents and those in position to hire (42%), frequent unemployment (40%), and loneliness (36%). Additionally, 22% reported their worst show business experiences were associated with being unable to find work, and 22% said that bombing was their worst experience.

Unemployment usually occurs "on the way up" and "on the way down" and those that occur on the way down are the worst. One goes from "being in demand" to "being at liberty". Jerry Lewis recounts that when his former partner, Dean Martin, came to his Muscular Dystrophy telethon unexpectedly after years of estrangement, all Jerry could think of to say was," Ya workin":?(p. 296)".

Sammy Davis, Jr. spoke of seeing Frank Sinatra during a severe downturn in Sinatra's career:

I couldn't take my eyes off of him {Sinatra}, walking the streets alone, an ordinary Joe who'd been a giant. He was fighting to make it back up again. By himself. The 'friends' were gone. He was walking slowly. A hundred people passed him in those few minutes, dozens who must have been fans who screamed for him only a few years before, but now nobody cared. . . And then I thought, My God, if it can happen to him, then how easily it could happen to me. This fragile acceptance could be shattered by a wrong move, or by complacence. The doors could start closing again (p. 48).

Stagefright is a nemesis for many performers including actors, classical musicians and dancers as well as popular performers. The symptoms of stagefright are both physical (sweating, vomiting, dizziness) and psychological (delusional thinking, amnesia, stupor). An attack of stagefright is often compared to dying: "I died out there;" "The audience is killing me." Some performers only experience stagefright prior to their performance while others are gripped in terror throughout their entire routine.

Stagefright is the result of the dynamic relationship between performer and audience. From the audience perspective the performer, whether a concert pianist or a juggler, is there to "entertain", that is, to transport audience members to that "great good place." In order to accomplish that the performer must project certainty and control. The audience demands the illusion of control and mastery from the performer. When a master magician's trick fails, he turns the failure into a joke played on the audience: "I fooled you; you thought I was going to make the rabbit disappear, but that's not the trick." Some magicians have developed very successful routines based on apparent failure. The audience is so relieved when they discover that the magician "failed" on purpose----it was all part of the act.

Performers must stand before their audiences defenseless except for their personas and their acts. Each audience is different. "Will they love me?" "Will they accept the illusion that I present?" Performing in spite of stagefright is a test of courage. The performer must be willing to fail. As Lawrence Olivier said, "You either battle or you walk away."

Performers do not often discuss stagefright; however, in the biographies 22% talked about bombing while an additional 30% mentioned the strategies they used to get primed to go on stage. These strategies included alcohol and drugs, sex, praying, self-hypnosis and eating. Pre-performance rituals might include a small alcoholic drink, a prayer, rubbing a magic talisman and hugs from entourage members.

When a show man perceives that he is bombing, there are only a few options available. One can retreat, i.e., leave the stage as did Richard Pryor. The performer may choose to "beg" the audience for love; this tack generally makes the audience uncomfortable. Some performers like Joan Rivers acted aggressively toward the audience, countering audience indifference with hostility. Finally, of course, the entertainer can simply soldier on, completing the routine.

Though there was broad general agreement on the rewards, benefits and problems associated with entertainment, emphasis differed according to the work orientation of the performers. In identifying entertainer orientations and placing performers in one of the three categories I looked for the following key factors:

a) reference group. Was the performer primarily concerned with pleasing the audience, other performers within the same speciality, and/or him/herself.
b) practice. How much time does the entertainer practice/rehearse? What does the show man practice?
c) failure. To what does the entertainer typically attribute failure?
d) success. To what does the entertainer attribute success? How does the entertainer respond to success?
e) self-identification. Does the performer identify himself primarily as an entertainer or as performer of his speciality, i.e., jazz musician, magician?

What follows is a discussion of the three fundamental entertainer orientations and the performers that can be most clearly identified with each orientation.

Performer-perfectionist. Approximately 12% of the sample clearly fit into this category. The jazz musicians, Art Hodes, Bud Freeman, Duke Ellington, Hampton Hawes, Eubie Blake, Earl Hines, and Ralph Sutton self identified as jazz musicians and their reference group consisted of others like themselves. They constantly worked on improving their skills; they tended to view their performances critically, always attempting to improve their musicianship. Two dancers, Norma Miller and Fred Astaire self-identified as dancers and constantly rehearsed. They, too, viewed their performances critically.

Both Clyde Beatty and Gunther Gebel-Williams self-identified as wild animals trainers. They brought in and trained new animals, developed new tricks and rehearsed continually. When performances went wrong, as they often did, Beatty and Williams blamed themselves rather than their animals.

No performer ever worked harder to perfect his magical effects than Houdini. He developed, rehearsed and presented novel tricks throughout his career. Many of his most spectacular effects were both dangerous and physically painful. He took special pleasure in developing effects which puzzled and amazed fellow magicians. A few other performers, at least during some periods in their lives, exhibited a strongly perfectionist orientation: Frank Sinatra, Nat Cole, Prince, Carol Lawrence.

The perfectionists self-identified with their speciality. They sought approval from others in their speciality, but beyond that, they considered themselves the best judges of their performances. They continuously worked on improving their acts. With some exceptions the perfectionists were less versatile and more strongly identified with their speciality than the other entertainers in the sample.

For perfectionists job satisfaction is strongly related to their evaluation of their skills. While they listed a number of positive aspects of show business, including travel, meeting famous people, and financial rewards, of first importance was the quality of their performances. Those who had almost complete control over the presentation of their acts like Houdini were more satisfied than those like Norma Miller or even Fred Astaire who worked with partners. Both Miller and Astaire complained about their partners, and

Sinatra frequently criticized, and sometimes refused to work with, certain conductors.

High on the list of job dissatisfaction was working conditions. A well rehearsed and choreographed act can only be satisfactorily presented when presentation space is acceptable. All the performers, particularly early in their careers, had to adjust to less than desirable conditions: poor lighting, inadequate stage, poor sound equipment, etc. As they became more successful, the entertainers were able to make demands about work conditions. Jazz musicians, were, however, generally an exception to that rule. Most of these musicians continued to perform in noisy, smoke-filled clubs. They frequently were forced to play popular music; often the only time they could *jam* with fellow jazz artists were after the clubs closed. Audience members were often drunk and would attempt to outloud the musicians. Even at the height of their careers, most jazz musicians had very little control over their work environment.

As a general rule perfectionists did not fear "bombing" as the success of their acts was rehearsed and audience reaction more predictable. More importantly, these perfectionists *knew* whether or not they had performed well so that audience reaction was less important to them than to those who identified as entertainers. Of course, no one likes to fail; and perfectionists enjoyed pleasing their audiences, but "if there is nobody in the club who understands jazz, so be it."

Perfectionists also frequently felt underappreciated by audience members, fellow performers, and venue owners. The hours of rehearsal, the intricacies of the performances, and the emotional and physical demands made on the performer, are generally not recognized by others. Only another dancer can fully appreciate the difficulty in executing certain steps. Perfectionists often made performing their acts look easy when, in fact, their execution was incredibly difficult. Perfectionists believed that they were grossly underpaid in comparison with performers whose acts made fewer technical demands.

The ranks of the perfectionist performer include both Blacks and Whites but only two females and one from T3. The majority were performing during the earliest time period when most of the jazz musicians were active.

Entertainer. During a trial Bill Cosby was asked his occupation; he stated unambiguously: "entertainer." Seventy-five percent of the sample saw themselves primarily as entertainers whose function is to entertain the audience. They viewed the audience as the arbiter of the quality of their performance. When they rehearsed, as they certainly did, the emphasis was on the effect on the audience rather than on the skill of the performance. They used their personas as an integral part of their acts, relying on the power of their personas to carry the audience with them.

For most entertainers, entertaining before a live audience was the central focus of their lives. They could not imagine another existence outside the footlights. Neil Diamond called performing "his ultimate orgasm in life when he walks out onto the stage and has a love affair with everybody in the audience (p. 195)." Sammy Davis, Jr. said:

> Part of show business is magic. You don't know how it happens. You don't know what circumstances are the ones that affect you.

> You don't know what the extra something is that makes you know they're with you, that puts that little straightner in your back and makes you know you can do it again (p. 337). . . . I felt the old familiar hunger. For fifty years I stood in the wings of theaters and clubs and felt the need to please the people, to stay with them until they love me. I felt that airiness in my chest that could only be filled by the people who were waiting for me (p. 388). Or as Milton Berle said:

> I'm . . . still running to the next show, coming alive under the lights, still making love to an audience that I know will go home and make love to one another and leave me alone again (p.352).

First and foremost the greatest satisfaction for entertainers was performing before an audience. Every performer in this category mentioned the joy of live performance; they agreed that it is the ultimate *high*. They exhibited a vitality, a zest which transmitted itself across the footlights. As Willie Nelson was quoted previously, it is the job of the entertainer to make the audience feel good. The entertainers' zest swept across the footlights, caught the audience and was reflected back on the performer. At the close of his show Al Jolson used to turn the house lights up in the theater so he could see the audience's faces. Feeling their approval Jolson would say, "You ain't heard noth'in yet" and sing for another hour.

The reference group for entertainers is the audience; consequently, their greatest fear is bombing. Every performance becomes a test; anything short of acceptance becomes rejection. The performer is either loved and accepted or not loved and rejected.

While entertainers often complained about working conditions, they generally felt capable of overcoming bad conditions. If they could be seen and heard, they could connect with their audiences. Ethel Merman, Fanny Brice and Sammy Davis, Jr. all believed that there were hardly any working conditions which they could not overcome. With or without a microphone Ethel Merman could be heard on the last row of the balcony.

Those who identified as entertainers were the most likely to suffer extreme stagefright and also to mention loneliness is a major problem. Each performance was an opportunity to experience either (a) the longed-for connection with the audience, or (b) the loneliness of rejection.

Mixed Motives. Approximately 13% of the sample evidenced a mixture of orientations toward entertaining.

Nothing Left to Lose. Several performers appeared to have begun a show business career because it was the best opportunity at the time. Heidi Mattson, Ward Hall, Trisha Yearwood, David Brenner, Tempest Storm, Hedy Jo Starr and Jett Williams are strong examples. Four out of the seven are associated with low status venues, strip clubs and outdoor show business.

Those in outdoor show business identified with others in that area. The title of Ward Hall's autobiography is **Struggle and Triumphs of a Modern Day Showman.** His proudest honor was his election as president of the **Independent Showman's Association.**

These performers worked hard, and some were successful; yet, the drive to entertain is missing. If you compare the autobiographies of Milton Berle or Jerry Lewis with that of David Brenner, you see the difference. Berle and Lewis lived to entertain; Brenner began his career as a writer and probably would have been satisfied with a career in writing, producing and directing.

This Little Light of Mine. A substantial number had goals associated with improving society or some segments of society, and they viewed their performances as allowing them to communicate these goals to an audience: Tupac Shakur, Joan Baez, Jim Morrison, Woody Guthrie, Lenny Bruce, Queen Latifah, Richard Pryor, Sam Kinison and Snoop Dogg.

Most of these entertainers had a political or social message that they wished to communicate: peace/anti-war, socialism, collectivism, anti-hypocrisy, and concerns about racism. Occasionally, their message interfered and harmed their careers; yet, most persisted. Joan Baez lost gigs because of her anti-war stance; Lenny Bruce, Sam Kinison and Richard Pryor lost gigs, were criticized in the press and sometimes had difficulty finding work because of the inflammatory content of their humor.

Queen Latifah's mother is an award winning educator who developed a number of successful esteem-building programs for inner-city children. Queen Latifah believes that her music and other endeavors can not only help build the self-esteem of young Black women, but can show them how to develop themselves. In her autobiography she emphasizes the importance of building a business: "Success is when opportunity meets preparation (p. 62)." The title of Snoop Dogg's autobiography, **The Times, Trials, and Hard-core Truths of Snoop Dogg,** points to his view that both his raps and his account of difficulties he has overcome, provide lessons for young Black males faced with similar life circumstances.

For musicians and song writers Woody Guthrie is the iconic performer who dedicated his career to the promulgation of his political beliefs; Joan Baez and Tupac Shakur followed in his footsteps. Lenny Bruce was the iconic comic who, like the court jester, ridiculed the ruling powers. Sam Kinison, Richard Pryor and Joan Rivers have followed his path. The performer who has a message to promote follows a difficult path. If the goal of entertainment is to please the audience, presenting a message that might not be well received creates a problem. Over time issue performers tend to *preach to the converted*; thus, they are often limited to small, self-selected audiences of true believers. It is difficult for an issue performer to find a mass audience. Finally, all successful entertainers must deal with fame. Most performers have a love/ hate relationship to fame, with love far exceeding hate.

Don't Rain on My Parade: Fame. Over 60% of the show people in this sample dealt with the issue of fame. Often they complained: their privacy was invaded; they had no time alone; fans were too demanding, etc. Yet, most went to great lengths to extend their allotted fifteen minutes. Those who could afford it hired press agents; others were their own press agents. While they complained about being mobbed by fans, they were highly affronted when they were unrecognized: "Don't you know who I am?" Chevy Chase's great line: "I'm Chevy Chase and you're not" epitomizes the attitude of most performers.

The word *fame* comes from the Latin and meant *manifest deeds*. Today it connotes widespread favorable notice. A celebrity is a well-known person and derives from the Latin term for festival/celebration. The cult of celebrity is nothing new; after all, Alexander the Great publicized his exploits; yet, it has certainly reached a peak in the beginning of the 21st century. Though changing technologies have contributed to the evolution of celebrity, the invention of the close-up speeded the process. Through the close-up movie audiences could gaze at a monster size picture of the star, her face blotting out everything else on the screen (Schickel 1985). Audiences wanted to know more about the star, and soon **Photoplay** (first published in 1910) and other movie magazines fed our insatiable thirst. Currently, **People, Us, Entertainment Tonight,** the tabloids and countless other media outlets bombard us with tidbits about the lives of entertainers.

Fans have a love/hate relationship with their idols. We want to be in their presence; we thrill to their touch, and yet we are angry with them for betraying our wanting. Our dreams of being accepted by the celebrity while realizing the unlikelihood of that happening makes us, the fans, resentful and angry (Schickel 1985; Lewis 1992). Sue Erickson Bloland (1999:52) has written perceptively about being the daughter of a famous man (Eric Erickson):

> When we grant another person the status of hero, we deny our own full potential for empowerment. Adulation dulls our awareness of the human dimensions of those we idealize, limiting our knowledge of them and of ourselves as human beings.

As the fan has a strongly ambivalent relationship with the celebrity, so has the celebrity with his/her fans. Marilyn Monroe (Schickel 1985) said:

> They {her fans} all want a chunk of you. A sex symbol becomes a thing. I just hate being a thing. When you are famous every weakness is exaggerated. It might be kind of a relief to be finished.

While the nature of fame and celebrity and their relationship to the motivation to entertain are explored in a forthcoming chapter, the importance of fame for show people requires emphasis. Both the performers themselves and their press agents devoted considerable effort to establish and then maintain name recognition. Joan Rivers said, "Everybody goes into this business for profit or recognition (p. 231)." Recognition takes a number of forms. Michael Jackson and his press agents were particularly gifted at piling on the hype. At one point Jackson complained because Elvis Presley was called "The King." Jackson asked his manager to start calling him "The King of Rock and Soul." In 1984 Elizabeth Dole (then Secretary of Transportation) agreed to "dream up" a

humanitarian award for Jackson if she could use his music from **Beat It** for a commercial about drunk driving. At the start of Jackson's **Victory Tour** the promoter, Don King, told the press:
Michael Jackson has transcended all earthly bounds. Every race, every color and creed is waiting for this tour. The way we shall lift the despairing and despondent enthralls me (p. 369).

During the filming of the **We Are the World** video, the camera focused on Jackson's Bass Weejun shoes and sequined socks. Jackson said, "People will know me as soon as they see the socks. . . Try taking footage of Bruce Springsteen's socks and see if anyone knows who they belong to (p. 412)."

Hampton Hawes felt that recognition/fame meant being the subject of a **This is Your Life.** Others thought being a headliner at a famous venue was the epitome of fame. As Eddie Fisher said, ". . . and the dream of seeing my name on the marquee of the **Paramount.** That dream came true (p. 372)." Richard Pryor said, "I want people to be able to recognize me by just looking at a nameless caricature and say, 'That's him; that's Richard Pryor!' Then I'll be great (Williams & Williams 1991:91-2)."

For almost all the show people in the sample, but most particularly for those who strongly self-identify as entertainers, fame is a major reward for pursuing a show business career. The loss of fame, anonymity, represents the downside. Bombing, unemployment and audience rejection are precursors to the loss of fame: anonymity. After his fall from being a number one box office attraction, the actor, Burt Reynolds, was quoted as saying, "I used to be Burt Reynolds." Recently, Patti LaBelle (Atlanta Journal/Constitution 6/26/2004) complained to the management of her hotel that the bellmen did not recognize her; she said, "…if it was Madonna, Celine or Britney Spears none of this would have happened."

In several of the preceding chapters, I have presented data on the childhood and early work experiences of those in the sample with a view toward understanding the processes by which they came to choose and develop their careers. In the following chapter I present data on the motive to entertain. The approach I take to motivation is primarily psychological, locating the need to act in the psyche of the individual. The motivational impetus to act and the socialization experiences of the individual interact to attract or repel a person toward certain career tracks.

CHAPTER ELEVEN
IF MY FRIENDS COULD SEE ME NOW:
THE MOTIVE TO ENTERTAIN

*More seductive than sex—More addictive than any drug—More precious than gold. (*Ad for the film, **Power**, Lorimar Productions)

Humans have always sought to understand why people behave as they do. First, novelists and biographers, then social scientists, sought to decipher the wellsprings of motivation. The concept "motive" can best be defined as ". . . the way behavior gets started, is energized, is sustained, is directed, and is stopped (McClelland 1985:5)." The terms motive and need are often used interchangeably, and various psychologists have identified core "motive/ needs", e.g., Maslow, Murray, Rogers, Freud.

While motivation has never been fundamental to sociology, a small number of scholars have made this concept central to their theoretical approaches. Max Weber (1964:98-99) defined motive as ". . . a complex of subjective meanings which seems to the actor himself or to the observer an adequate ground for the conduct in question." The early American sociologist, W. I. Thomas (1969) said that motives" impelled toward action" and identified his famous four wishes: security, new experience, response and recognition. However, interest in motivation as a "state that impelled toward action" gradually declined in sociology as the position articulated by C. Wright Mills, who argued that sociologists should focus on peoples' explanations of their behavior, gained adherents.

A number of contemporary psychologists have identified and measured what are often called *social motives*, chief among which are achievement, power and affiliation/intimacy. David McClelland and his students have concentrated on the study of the "need for achievement" (nAch) (McClelland 1985).McAdams has studied intimacy and Winter the need for power. Figure 1 illustrates the defining characteristics of these three social motives. Those who are high on nAch are primarily concerned with mastery and the attainment of excellence and are generally entrepreneurial. People high on the need for affiliation/intimacy (nAff) desire closeness, interpersonal warmth, and self-disclosure, but under threat can turn prickly and self-protective (McAdams 1982).

Figure 1: The Social Motives

	NEED FOR:	IDENTIFYING CHARACTERISTICS
ACHIEVEMENT (N ACH) N	Moderate Challenge	Entrepreneurship/Sales
	Improve Performance	
	Positive Orientation Toward Work	
POWER (N P) N	Performance Feedback	Office Holding
	Having Impact	Power Related Careers
	Maintaining Reputation	Entertainment
	Arousing Strong Emotions	Psychology
		Journalism
		Business Management
		Clergy
		Prestige Possessions: Credit Cards
		Colors: Red & Black
		Peak Experiences Defined in Power Tier 1
		Sycophants
		Extreme Risk Takers
AFFILIATION/ INTIMACY (n Aff) N	Establish, Restore, Maintain	Avoid Conflict
	Positive Affective Relations	Sensitive to Facial Cues
	Closeness, Warmth, Communication	

David Winter has focused on the need for power (nPower) and defines it as ". . . having impact on others, arousing strong emotions in others, or maintaining reputation and prestige (Winter 1988:510)." Npower predicts a multiplicity of actions including choosing occupations where one has the opportunity to "command attention and dazzle others", acquiring "prestige" possessions and surrounding one's self with lesser known followers. Those with a high need for power also prefer large crowds, are easily flattered by subordinates, but can be exceptional leaders who can rally the troops and lead the charge (Winter 1988; McClelland 1985; Zarbreggan 2000). Npower people are extreme risk takers and more interested in attracting attention than winning.

Status loss is a paramount threat which usually precipitates self-destructive behaviors like alcohol and drug abuse. Among men, but not women, nPower is also strongly associated with the *expansive profligate impulse* which includes alcohol and drug abuse, verbal and physical aggression, gambling, and exploitive sexuality (Winter 1988; Zarbreggen 2000). Their fear of loss of visibility, of recognition, of fame leads some of those high in nPower to behavioral excesses which, in turn, makes them less employable.

In contrast to nAch, research on child rearing practices which produce nPower adults is limited; however, three factors are identified: parental permissiveness for sexual and physical aggression and concern with table manners (McClelland 1985; Winter & Carlson 1988). With only a few exceptions the data are too limited to determine the prevalence of these practices in the childhoods of the show people in the sample.

At its most fundamental level the need for power may be conceptualized as the need for attention: "see me, watch me, look what I'm doing." The giving and receiving of attention have been studied by sociobiologists (Chance & Larsen 1976) and the sociologist, Charles Derber (1981) who points out that every society provides rules of attention giving and seeking. For example, women in Western societies are typically attention giving to both men and children. The wife introduces conversation topics and supports topics which focus attention on the husband. Or, in an organization, the subordinate (either male or female) directs attention to the boss. Even though we have rules for attention giving and getting, Derber (1981:22) notes that some have greater needs to be the center of attention than others, and he argues that "conversational narcissism is the key manifestation of the dominate attention getting psychology in America."

You're the Top: nPower. Psychologists have developed methods for measuring the three social motives (McAdams 1982; Winter & Stewart 1978; McClelland 1985). Any extended piece of narrative can be coded for nAch, Aff, and Power. The system for coding these motives was first developed for use with the Thematic Apperception Test (TAT) and then redefined for an extended narrative. The scorer identifies themes in the narrative which represent the three social motives. The scoring manual provides the key words and images for each social motive. For example, a statement like, "I wanted to learn the most difficult magic tricks" would illustrate nAch while a sentence such as "I held the audience in the palm of my hand" illustrates nPower. The coder calculates the number of images or statements for each motive and divides by the number of words in the text so that scores reflect images per 1000 words.

My sample contained 50 autobiographies. All the autobiographies were "co-authored" by professional writers; however, these writers work from tapes made by the subjects. These tapes are usually supplemented by interviews in which the subjects' responses are recorded. Consequently, most of the content of these autobiographies consists of direct quotations from their subjects, organized by the professional writer.

I coded these autobiographies for images and statements reflecting the three social motives. The scores for the sample reflect the number of images per 1000 words. A few samples of the statements used to identify the social motives provide a flavor of the material in the texts.

nPower.

I guess I wanted people to pay attention to me, to love me, so I stopped hiding. Eddie Fisher (p. 10).
When Elizabeth and I first married, my career was at least as important as hers, and I earned much more than she did. Now the roles were reversed . My career was at a standstill. Eddie Fisher (p. 213).
I ordered twenty-five boxes to get Irving Kaye started. The total bill, including some last-minute shopping in the luggage department, brought the whole megillah to $4,200. Sure, I was at twenty-two already owning two Cadillacs, and a Jaguar XKE, and spending more on others than myself. Gold watches, bracelets, lighters, rings. But I was feeling high and mighty and unstoppable . . . Jerry Lewis (p. 153).

> It made me understand that you can do a great deal in three-quarters of a lifetime and never really know the impact you've had on so many. Jerry Lewis (p. 307).

nAch

> And you want to know if I still practice? That's the least I can do for what I've gotten. As my doctor once told me, 'I haven't arrived; I practice medicine.' Me too. I haven't arrived. Just making the trip daily. Art Hodes (p. 28).

> He laid it out straight. 'I've been teaching vocal for quite some time. I gave up teaching piano except in the one or two cases where the student is prepared to work at it seriously. I'll take you on, but believe me, you're going to have to really work, and work hard, just to catch-up to where you should be at this stage of your career. It isn't going to be easy and you can quit any time. But if you stick with me, I'll teach you.' I was determined . . . you can bet I'd stick. Art Hodes (p. 37)

nAff.

> When we first started dating, he used to ask me what would make me happy. I said, 'First of all, a home and happy children—preferably in the quiet seclusion of the country, with lots of lawn and trees and peace and love.' Carol Lawrence (p. 94).

> I lived for those beautiful, intimate moments. Being with Bobby was my only happiness, and oh' how I clung to him, physically and emotionally. How warm and safe I felt when we were together. Carol Lawrence (p.92).

I coded the autobiographies for statements reflecting the three social motives. However, in order to assess the strength of the motives, I needed a comparison group. In their book on American elites Lerner and co-authors (1996) compared motive scores among a random sample of elites including television, media and film leaders. None of the respondents in the Lerner samples were performers but rather writers, producers and directors. Using the elites' responses to a set of five TAT pictures, Lerner and collaborators found that the "new cultural elite" {media leaders} had lower average or mean achievement (5.66) but higher power (7.80) and intimacy scores (3.35) than the business elite.

The scores on nPower for the entertainer sample ranged from 8.76 to 15.01, with a mean of 10.02. Among those scoring significantly above the mean were Joan Baez, Milton Berle, Snoop Dogg, Lenny Bruce, Sammy Davis, Jr., Eddie Fisher, George Jones, Jerry Lewis, Reba McEntire, John Phillips and Joan Rivers.

Among those above the mean on nPower both Joan Baez and Lenny Bruce were primarily concerned with their effect on people's attitudes and beliefs. The title of Bruce's autobiography, **How to Talk Dirty and Influence People,** speaks to his concern about influencing public opinion. He repeats verbatim much of the court testimony in many of his legal skirmishes and lists all "80 on" prominent public figures that signed a statement on his behalf.
Most of those who were high in nPower recounted their successes and also their fears at losing visibility. In a recent interview Jerry Lewis (Kaplan 2000:50) discussed his career:

> I don't give a shit if people think I have a fantastic ego. I earned it! I worked my heart out! And you know what? I'm as good as they get.

Or

> Now here's what Hollywood fears and hates: multifacetedness. You see they don't particularly care that you write and produce and direct and act. What they care about is that by your doing all that you punctuate how singularly faceted they are. (Kaplan 2000:55).

Lewis (Kaplan 2000:63) discussed his fear of loss of fame, of celebrity:

> I can't take Jerry Lewis out in front of fifty people for free! What would that do to his psyche? I have to protect and defend Jerry Lewis! He's nine years old and I have to live with him.

The range of achievement scores for the entertainer sample was 4.05 to 7.78 with a mean of 5.53, just slightly below the mean for Lerner's media elites. Beatty, Williams, Miller, Freeman, Rapp, Latifah and Hodes) scored above the mean in nAch. Both Beatty and Williams reported on their efforts to dominate their animals; however, both also spoke at length concerning their struggles teaching their animals new and path-breaking feats. The jazz musicians and dancer continuously tried to improve their musical skills throughout their careers. The importance of both achievement and power are expressed in Freeman's (p.84) comment about playing jazz concerts: "It's a marvelous feeling: it's the greatest ego trip in the world. This is what jazz soloists have been waiting for all our lives."

The range of nAff scores for the entertainers was from 2.85 to 9.01 with a mean of 3.45, very similar to the score for Lerner's media elites. Those who were above the mean include Judy Collins, Phyllis Newman, Melissa Manchester and Carol Lawrence. The title of Judy Collins' autobiography, **Trust Your Heart,** illuminates the thrust of her book as well as the content of Newman's, Manchester's and Lawrence's. These women speak at great length about their relationships with various lovers, husbands and family members.

In sum, the entertainers score higher than the media elites on nPower while approximating the scores of the media elites on nAff and nAch. Many of those who scored at or above the mean on nAch were Black musicians, and only female entertainers scored above the mean on nAff. The mean score on nPower was highest in the second period (T2) because of the number of jazz musicians working during that time. All in all results from this limited sample confirms the theory that entertainers are motivated by a high need for power, supporting the view of Dabbs et al (1990)and Fisher & Fisher (1981) (reported previously) that comics exhibit self-aggrandizement and need for control and dominance.

The misbehavior of entertainers continues to make headlines. Alcohol and drug addictions, sexual promiscuity, and over-the-top public excesses continue as staples of newspaper, tabloid and television features. Pundits are asked to explain why so many entertainers violate the standards of public deportment. As history has shown, the violation of societal norms has been part of the behavior of entertainers across cultures and throughout history. Strangers and sojourners in their own and foreign cultures, they were allowed to transgress norms (Merriam 1964). Their work environments are conducive to alcohol and drug use and promiscuity. Beyond these important factors in explaining entertainer deviance, might there be a psychological component?

Dance Ten: Looks Three: The Expansive Profligate Impulse. McClelland and Winters have argued that those high in nPower may develop the expansive profligate impulse (hereafter EPI). Individuals who have a high need for power but lack internal control often engage in a variety of excessive, usually self-destructive behaviors like alcohol or illicit drug use, sexual promiscuity, physical and verbal aggression and gambling (Winter 1988). Winter found that while the EPI was common among men, it was rare for women.

All 117 books were coded for alcohol abuse (sustained use which interfered with performance and/or personal relationships, substance abuse (sustained use which interfered with performance and/or personal relationships), gambling (sustained losses which caused severe financial problems). I did not code for physical aggression because I was not confident that biographers or their subjects would record the frequency with which spouses, children or others were assaulted.

Coding for sexual promiscuity was difficult because of the ambiguity in the data. Some entertainers confessed in general terms to sexual promiscuity, e.g., Eddie Fisher, Waylon Jennings. A few listed a number of lovers, i.e., Tempest Storm while some biographers spoke in general terms of rumors of sexual promiscuity concerning the entertainer profiled. The indicator I used for sexual promiscuity was the admission by the entertainer or the biographer that the person had a large number of sexual partners over an extensive period of their careers.

In order to identify EPI in my sample I added two behaviors: binging and "living large." Food is often problematic for entertainers as they must be concerned with their physical appearance. Excessive food intake can be a substitute for alcohol or substance abuse or confounded with them. While a number of show people were binge eaters, none indicated that they binged and purged so I coded for binge eating.

As noted, one of the characteristics of those who have a high need for power is the collection of status possessions; so I coded for evidence of "living large", i.e., spending significantly beyond one's financial resources. Altogether, I used six indices of EPI: alcohol abuse, substance abuse, sexual promiscuity, gambling, binging and living large.

For the sample as a whole 39% had severe alcohol problems, 25% abused illicit drugs, 28% were sexually promiscuous, 12% binged, 14% were problem gamblers and 22% lived large. Of the 117 entertainers, 26 (22.2%) exhibited three or more behaviors associated with EPI. Of the 26 four were women, 10 were Black and one was of mixed race. Five were comics; the remainder was singers. None of the relatively unknown show people exhibited three or more EPI behaviors. The 26 were distributed fairly evenly throughout the three time periods. Of the 26 ten were physically incapacitated or died prematurely: Lenny Bruce, Jim Morrison, Freddie Prinze, Sam Cooke, Sam Kinison, Hank Williams, Dennis Wilson, Tupac Shakur, Richard Pryor and Janis Joplin.

Most of those who abused alcohol and/or drugs started with alcohol; many like Hank Williams started getting drunk as adolescents. Alcohol and substance abuse usually begin when the performer's career is ascending. Roman and Blum (1982) point out that the use of alcohol and other mood-altering substances facilitate the belief that one is in control, performing more than adequately. Each time the performer steps on stage, he has the potential to fail. The effects of some drugs, particularly the opiates, mask the numbing fear of failure. Stimulants allow the user to keep going beyond the point of normal exhaustion. Performers on tour frequently use stimulants to keep going and "downers" to decompress.

A number of performers died from alcohol or illicit drugs or problems associated with their use including Lenny Bruce, Janis Joplin, Dennis Wilson, Freddie Prinze, Hank Williams, W. C. Fields, Billie Holiday and Jim Morrison. Others managed to pull themselves together and escape the downward spiral: Etta James, Jerry Lewis, George Jones and John Phillips.

Sexual promiscuity is facilitated in the work environments of show people, and it is doubtful if any of the show folks in the sample remained absolutely faithful to their spouses; however, a number clearly reveled in promiscuity and evidenced little concern for circumspection for the sake of the spouses, children or careers: Tempest Storm, Waylon Jennings, Chico Marx, Eddie Fisher, Milton Berle, B.B. King, Frank Sinatra, Patsy Cline, Jerry Lewis. For example, B.B. King speaks forthrightly about his "love for women"; he acknowledges fathering 15 children. He says that if a woman claims a child is his, he never denies it. Sam Cooke began his career as a gospel singer, but upon moving to California, he started serious drinking (a quart of Chevis Regal a night) and recruiting sexual partners. He was murdered in a motel where he had an assignation with a prostitute.

Only a few entertainers reported spending inordinate amounts of money on gambling. However, the incidence of excessive gambling may be under-reported. However, Al Jolson, Milton Berle, Clyde Beatty, George Jones, Liberace, Oliver Hardy, Chico Marx and Eddie Fisher all wagered more than they could afford.

While many performers complained about having to constantly monitor their weight, a substantial number evidenced severe, and often life long problems with food: Jackie Gleason, Sam Kinison, Oliver Hardy, Etta James, Joan Rivers, B.B. King, Patsy Cline, Louie Anderson, Fats Waller, Patti LaBelle, Queen Latifah and Gilda Radner. These performers had weight problems as children. While a few were able to control their weight, most could not. As Etta James said, "Food started earliest and lasted longest." Binge eating is similar to binge drinking. The binger abstains for awhile and then loses control. Louie Anderson describes binge eating:

> After a few minutes I decided not to fight the urge any longer. I was hungry. Starving. I had to eat something. Anything. The worst thing you can do to yourself is to snack at night, especially late at night. I know. . . It's as if I'm in a horror movie, controlled by a mysterious force emanating from the refrigerator. Night of the Living Bingers.

Patsy Cline, Gilda Radner and Joan Rivers managed to control their food intake; the others were unable. B.B. King and Patti LaBelle became diabetic. In spite of entreaties of family, friends and agents, Louie Anderson, Jackie Gleason, Fats Waller and Oliver Hardy largely quit trying to control their weight. And, of course, for Gleason, Anderson, Kinison, Hardy and Waller, being fat was part of their personas. A slim Oliver Hardy or Jackie Gleason would have altered the carefully honed personas beloved by their fans.

The stars made astronomical sums of money; yet, many lived relatively conservatively: Jack Benny, Fred Allen, W. C. Fields, Dinah Shore, Edgar Bergen. While these people lived rather modestly, many spent more money than even they could afford. The biographies were replete with examples of the spending habits of Frank Sinatra, Eddie Fisher, Sammy Davis, Jr., Jackie Gleason, Tupac Shakur and Michael Jackson. Homes and estates, jewelry for wives and lovers, entourages, transportation (private limousines and airplanes) and grand gestures (flying an entourage to Europe for a vacation) made up the bulk of the big spenders' major expenses. The grand gesture is particularly appreciated: tipping the valet parking attendant $100, hosting 200 people at a private banquet. Stars have difficulty scaling back their living standards even when bankruptcy threatens. They may find themselves in a downward spiral, propelled by alcohol and/ or drugs and out-of-control spending. Waylon Jennings said:

> Lying there, I started thinking about what I'd won after ten years of banging around this honky-tonk circuit. My health was shot. I was nearly close to a quarter of a million dollars in debt, and getting deeper in the hole whether I played shows or not. . . I was paying alimony to three wives. If I went on the road I lost money. If I stayed home I lost money (p. 171).

What follows are brief biographies of three well-known entertainers who exhibited three or more of the behaviors identified with the EPI.

Jackie Gleason. As a boy Gleason was plump, and as he aged, he continued to gain weight. At one time he weighed 285 pounds; yet, his weight became a part of his persona, both as Jackie Gleason, the Great One, and his alter ego, Ralph Kramden. Gleason denied he was an alcoholic but rather a drunk as:"drunks don't go to meetings." Gleason was also promiscuous, especially during his first marriage. He surrounded himself with large entourages, frequently transporting them across country. He provided food and drink for friends and strangers. His largess was acknowledged among show people, and he never disappointed.

Tupac Shakur. At 25 Tupac Shakur was murdered while riding in the BMW driven by Marlon (Suge) Knight, the head of **Death Row Records.** Shakur's family background involved black activism (His mother was a member of the **Black Panthers**; nevertheless, he went to a school of performing arts in Baltimore. He left home for California when he was 17. In 1991 **Interscope Records** released his first "gangsta" rap album. Others in the rap music business criticized Shakur for not being "authentic", that is not being a genuine gangster. He began carrying weapons and training. He had *Thugs Life* tattooed across his stomach. As he became well known, his range of acquaintances extended to include celebrities and their entourages. Young women sought his company, and record promoters, agents and producers paid his bills.

In this fast company, he was drinking and using marijuana constantly. His legal troubles mounted; he was wounded in a shooting and was convicted in another case and sentenced to jail. While he was in prison, **Interscope** advanced Shakur $600,000 which was soon used up by lawyers and his 20 dependents. With the help of Suge Knight, Shakur was finally released from prison. He began working 19 hours a day while consuming prodigious amounts of alcohol and marijuana. He lived large: diamond encrusted medallions, four Rolls Royces, as well as an abundance of female companionship. While riding with Suge Knight, he was murdered. To date his murderer has not been identified.

Jim Morrison. From adolescence Jim Morrison began to explore his consciousness. He read Blake, Rimbaud, and, especially, Aldous Huxley's **The Doors of Perception** which introduced him to the effects of psychedelics. As Morrison wrote in his diary, "I won't come out; you must come to me . . . where

I can construct a universe within the skull to rival the real (p. 50)." He first used marijuana and then LSD as "doors to perception." He believed that the source of his poetry and music were these drugs. He also used amyl nitrates and alcohol.

As Morrison and his group, **The Doors**, became successful, he started using drugs in front of the audience. His timing and enunciation began to falter. His solution was to increase his consumption. Jim and **The Doors** were branded as troublemakers. They were banned from the very popular **Ed Sullivan Show** and missed performances while on the road. To test his power over audiences, Morrison decided to start a riot. He succeeded. More riots followed. With each riot Morrison's contempt for his audience mounted. The beginning of his downward spiral was probably the night that Morrison addressed his audience:

> What are you doing here? Well, man we can play music all night, but that's not what you really want, is it? You want something else, something more, something greater than you've ever seen before, right? Well, fuck you. We came to play music (p. 215).

Much like Lenny Bruce's last years, Morrison's were dominated by criminal charges at both the state and federal level. And, like Bruce, Morrison was self-absorbed with his legal struggles. He finally bottomed out in New Orleans.

> Everyone who was there saw it, man. He lost all his energy about midway through the set. He hung on to the microphone and it just slipped away. You could actually see it leave him... The Doors never again appeared in public as a quartet (p.330).

Morrison died shortly thereafter.

A substantial number of the entertainers in this sample evidenced a high need for power, and 22% presented three or more behaviors associated with EPI, a psychological condition which results when a person with a high need for power loses self-control. The culture industry in general and show business in particular, present the occupational practitioner with ample opportunities to engage in EPI related behaviors. Further, their work environments provided very little structure. More importantly, many of the people around them rarely discouraged their harmful behaviors, or, as was often the case, actually encouraged these behaviors.

One of the primary functions of the entourage is to tell the star "everything is okay: getting drunk or stoned, missing gigs, insulting the audience is all okay." The entourage masks the entertainer's insecurities, but at a heavy price. As long as the performer can pay the tab, the entourage will continue to say, "…everything is coming up roses."

Even more problematic for the entertainer than the entourage is the audience. Audience members frequently encourage performers' bad behaviors. Janis Joplin, Richard Pryor, Jim Morrison, Hank Williams, Tupac Shakur and Lenny Bruce, among others, were rewarded for bad behavior. The audience cheered when Morrison exposed himself in front of them, or Bruce and Pryor described the details of their drug use. When Richard Pryor stopped using illicit drugs, his audience deserted him. His open defiance of drug laws had become part of his persona, and his audience demanded that he not change. As Pryor's relationship with his audience changed, he gradually withdrew from stand-up.

In the brief concluding chapter, I summarize the findings of this study and relate them to the work environment in the culture industry.

CHAPTER TWELVE
THE ROAR OF THE GREASEPAINT: THE 5 CRISES OF THE ENTERTAINER

With increased free time, educational attainment and technological innovations, the importance of leisure activities in western societies has expanded. Key to the production of leisure pursuits are *artists* who create products which various publics consume. In the fine arts painters, novelists, sculptors and performance artists develop content which a well-educated and affluent public enjoys. Popular entertainers also consider themselves significant members of the arts community, those creative individuals who produce and perform cultural *content (Florida* 2002; Caves 2000). In this concluding chapter I address the stresses and strains on live performers in the popular arts in relation to the structural and cultural conditions inherent in the culture industry.

The World on a String: Live Popular Performance and the Culture Industry. As discussed in the Introduction, there are several key characteristics of employment in the culture industry: an excess of aspirants over available jobs, lack of defined career paths, absence of agreed-upon standards of job performance, absence of defined tenure tracks, and dependence upon non-colleagues, e.g., the audience, critics, producers, etc. for job approval and rewards, hence reputation is the key ingredient in defining success (Caves 2000; Florida 2002; Bielby & Bielby 1999; Giuffree 1999; Menger 1999).

In consequence the choice of work in the culture industry entails considerable risk and continuous anxiety; yet, many choose it, and of those many make a life-long commitment. Several theories have been advanced to explain this seeming conundrum. Work in the culture industry may offer a route of upward mobility (Gideon & Sjoberg 1957); culture workers make a probabilistic miscalculation in which they believe that *if they pay their dues* they will eventually achieve success (Menger 1999) and, finally, the theory of equalizing differences which posits that one very strong, positive motivating factor can override negative considerations (Rosen 1986).

For culture workers the powerful motivating factor is their belief that they have *the gift,* the unique ability to create and/or perform art which nourishes and sustains the human species. Those who are given *the gift* have an obligation to cultivate and share it with others, to do otherwise is to dishonor *the gift* and the giver, whomever that might be, e.g., the gods, fate, etc. Sometimes *the gift* is from the devil; there are many folk tales and stories about artists who have sold their souls to the devil or, alternately, jousted with him, i.e., Faust, the blues musician Robert Johnson. The biographies of producers of serious art, e.g., classical composers and musicians, painters, serious novelists, etc. attest to the struggles most of these artists undergo in order to practice their art. We have grown accustomed to the portrayal of the *struggling artist* who sacrifices his/her family, health and often sanity for art's sake. We are more likely to view the popular performer as that person is portrayed in the media: hedonistic, self-destructive, without any artistic integrity. The findings of this study suggest otherwise.

With a Little Bit of Luck: The Five Crises of the Artist/Entertainer. Philip Ennis (1993) described the major dilemmas of the artist. He argued that the primary challenge for the artist is to deal with "the gift." In order to transmit that gift, the artist must develop the skill required to effectively present that gift: "It is the combination of the gift and the skill which makes the artist. Gift only leaves frustration or tragedy; skill only yields artisan/craftsman (Ennis 1993:16)."

Based on the relationship between the artist and the gift, Ennis posited five crises faced by the artist as she moves through her career.

Ennis described the five crises of the artist, the first being "Do I have it?" This concern develops early in the artistic career. The majority of this sample began public performing in childhood, and they generally interpreted their early success with audiences as a sign that *they had it.* As evidenced in their early careers they sought validation for the presence of the gift: audience response, praise from agents, mentors, and established stars. Some were temporarily discouraged, but they persisted, always seeking further confirmation.

The second crisis is, "Can I do it?" For some in the sample, building requisite skills required long hours of practice, e.g., Art Hodes, Clyde Beatty, Fred Astaire, Duke Ellington. These performers, usually musicians and dancers, often began their careers by studying with professional instructors and/or prolonged apprenticeships. Their teachers and mentors were key in confirming their gift.

However, most learned performance skills by doing. Comics, singers and variety artists rarely studied with professionals; rather they honed their acts while actively performing before the public. They learned how to build an act, develop a persona and master timing through trial and error. Audience approval represented validation.

The third crisis is, "Can I show it?" As previously noted, the relationship between entertainer and audience is always problematic. The jazz musician may have a high skill level and be musically creative and yet not be able to communicate those qualities to an audience. A magician can possess a high skill level and yet not transmit magical mystery to others. Audiences are not impressed by technical skill; they attend performances to be entertained. If they are not, the performer fails. If any performer is to succeed, he/she must relate to the audience. The most successful ventriloquist of the 20th century, Edgar Bergen, was unskilled (moved his lips) and yet was a huge success in several media, including, however improbable, radio.

The fourth crisis is, "Can I do it again?" The jazz performer sits down at the piano; maybe he is solo, perhaps part of a trio. He must pick a melody, **Take the A Train,** and improvise. His audience must believe that they are hearing something new, something fresh, something no one has ever heard before. Can he do it again? He did it last night, but this is tonight. With each audience singers like Waylon Jennings and Willy Nelson must sing "their greatest hits" as if for the first time.

The great comics, Lenny Bruce and Richard Pryor, essentially riffed on a theme. Last night the audience howled with laughter; will they tonight. Perhaps a few performers, e.g., Jack Benny, Al Jolson, finally came to feel secure; they believed that their relationship with their audience was so primal that it could not be disrupted, but the majority always recognized the possibility of failure. The only ones who didn't fear failure were those who ceased to care or never cared. Many of the burlesque comics described by Salutin (1973) had long ceased to make an effort to entertain. They took up space and filled time. Lawrence Olivier played the English music hall comic (**The Entertainer**) who had given up trying to entertain; Olivier played him doing his routine while occasionally glancing down at his watch:"How many more minutes do I have to fill?"

The bane of entertainers, stagefright, is the almost inevitable result of the requirement to perform "the gift" over and over again, night after night, year after year. Never can the performer feel secure; as long as she does her act. The possibilities of failure and rejection are always there.

The final crisis is, "When do I quit?" For most in this sample, the answer has been *never*. Very few ever voluntarily retire. They change their acts, modify their personas, await a revival, or play in increasingly less desirable venues. Even when they become sucker sore, they soldier on. From their biographies and especially their autobiographies, one might expect at least some of the performers to ruminate on the difficulties of maintaining a performing career into mature or old age. They do not. Most believe, or wish to believe, that they still have "the gift." When Al Jolson's career was reborn because of the success of **The Jolson Story**, he refused to credit Larry Parks, the actor who played him. Instead, it was clear to him that his new audience recognized the presence of "the gift." For others past their prime, the belief that a new audience will recognize "the gift" helps the performers through lean times. Currently, Neil Diamond is experiencing a comeback; he's playing Las Vegas and his music is selling. If it can happen to him, it can happen to anyone. Several other performers in the sample were said to have retired or whose career had peaked, but have revived, e.g., Mariah Carey, Garth Brooks, Etta James. Bill Cosby has morphed into a public lecturer/scold. One of the few entertainers who quit at the height of his career was Artie Shaw {not in the sample} who walked out on his spectacularly successful career when he was only 44. He said of his early success and his decision to disband his band and join the navy:

> I was reaping the whirlwind. When you are in the process of becoming a major star, you lose your sanity. . . It amazes me that anybody goes through it sane. It took me a war and two psychoanalyses (Shaw 1999:80).

As previously documented, some in the sample did not stay sane. They either self-destructed or engaged in behaviors that ruined their health and emotional well-being.

On a Clear Day You Can See Forever: The Future of Live Performance.
Increasingly, popular entertainment is mass-mediated as new technology
delivers cultural content through many and varied platforms. Is there a
future for live performance? Producers as well as the artists themselves are
learning how to integrate live performance with mass-mediated technological
innovations.

At the beginnings of the recording industry performers sold their records
during their performances and also hand-delivered them to radio stations,
using their persuasive skills to induce the station manager to plug the songs.
Their live performances sold the songs, and radio play sold future bookings.
Today musicians and singers must tour to sell their music. Some artists have
industry representatives who plug the songs and generate *buzz* about the
new tour or recording. Yet, many artists do their own promotions, distribute
their recordings and book their own tours. Comics, variety artists, and
dancers have learned to market themselves. Magicians tour magic clubs and
sell their demonstration videos, and variety artists market videos to fellow
artists and fans. The Internet has freed the artist from dependence on large
media corporations; the performer can communicate with fans without an
intermediary.

However, the entertainer still must tour; careers cannot be developed or
sustained without direct audience contact. Magicians, mimes, and professional
ballroom dancers tour clubs and halls delivering their acts, meeting their
fans and selling their videos. Even though the business of show business has
changed in response to technological innovations, the connection between
showman/woman and audiences persists.

The Smell of the Crowd. The findings from this study suggest that live
entertainment has changed dramatically over the last 150 years while
remaining remarkably unchanged. From the beginning of human society,
shamans danced, sang, told stories and made the gods speak. The same acts
that we appreciate today were practiced by shamans and, eventually, full time
performers.
One of the significant changes that has occurred in the approximately 150
years encompassing this study is the change in the demographic composition
of entertainers. Overall, there has been a significant increase in participation
of minority group members in entertainment, particularly Black women.
Also, there would seem to be an increase in the number of performers who
identify as biracial. In show business in general women have often participated
significantly. Once religious strictures were loosened, women were recruited

for theatrical productions where they often achieved numerical parity with men. However, men have predominated in music, comedy and variety. Women are increasingly active as comedians and soloists; however, men still predominate in music and variety.

Slowly, the educational level of entertainers and their parents has increased as well as the occupational attainment level of the performers' fathers. Religious participation continues to be an important factor in the lives of entertainers and their families. Religious institutions are still training grounds for beginning performers.

This research identifies a common path followed by the majority of performers, whether famous or unknown:

---

a) early childhood experience performing before live audiences;
b) these first experiences rewarded either financially or emotionally;
c) experiential learning;
d) encouragement and direction from significant others, e.g., family
   members, agents, established stars, colleagues.

The data from the autobiographies suggest that these entertainers may have a high need for power (nPower). These show people continue to perform as long as they are physically able in spite of the emotional demands of public performing. Many succumb to self-destructive behaviors.
Unlike Artie Shaw the show folks in this sample reflected the lyrics of the great show business anthem,

There's No Business Like Showbusiness:
I wouldn't trade it for a pot of gold/
On with the Show.

APPENDIX A
Showbusiness Biographies

Adler, Bill. (1986). *The Cosby Wit: His Life and Humor.* Carroll & Graf Publ.

_____ (1987). *Sinatra: The Man and the Myth.* Bill Adler Books.

Anderson, Louie. (1993). *Godly Jumbo: Hello Cruel Work.* Viking.

Bacon, James. (1985). How *Sweet It Is: The Jackie Gleason Story.* St. Martin's Press.

Baez, Joan. (1987). *And A Voice to Sing With: A Memoir.* Summit Books.

Beatty, Clyde. (1965). *Facing the Big Cats: My World of Lions and Tigers.* Doubleday.

Berenson, Jan.(1997). *Will Power: A Biography.* Pocket Books.

Bergen, Candice. (1984). *Knock On Wood.* Simon & Schuster.

Berle, Milton. (1974). *Milton Berle.* Dell.

Boley, Bill. (1997). My *Life in Magic and Ventriloquism.* Hopkinsville, KY.

Bone, Howard. (2001). *Side Show: My Life with Geeks, Freaks and Vagabonds in the Carney Trade.* Sun Dog Press.

Bowman, Jeffrey. (1995). *The Totally Unauthorized Biography of Whitney Houston.* Harper Collins.

Brenner, David.(1983). *Soft Pretzels and Mustar*d. Berkley Books.

Brown, Gary. (1997). *The Coney Island Fakir: The Magical Life of Al Flosso.* L & L Co.

Bruce, Lenny.(1966). *How to Talk Dirty and Influence Peo*ple. Playboy Press.

Carroll, Diahann.(1986). *Diahann!* Ivy Books.

Cassidy, Bruce.(1979). *Dinah! An Intimate Biography.* Berkley Books.

Chablis, Lady. (1996). *The Lady Chablis: Hiding My Candy.* Pocket Books.

Collins, Judy. (1987). *Trust Your Heart.* Fawcett.

Cooper, Daniel. (1995). *Lefty Frizzell: The Honky Tonk Life of Country Music's Greatest Singer*. Little Brown.

Daly, Marsha. (1978). Peter *Frampton*. Grosset & Dunlap.

Dana, Stanley. (1977). *The World of Earl Hines*. Scribner.

Davis, Sammy Jr. (1989). *Why Me? The Sammy Davis Jr. Story*. Warner Books.

Doggy, Snoop. (1999). *Snoop Doggy: The Times and Hard-Core Truths of Snoop Dogg*. Wm. Morrow.

Echols, Alice. (1999). *Scars of Sweet Paradise: The Life and Times of Janis Joplin*. Henry Holt.

No author or publishing date given. *Bad Boys: The Real Story Behind America's Hot Rebels----- Eminem*. Publ.

Etheridge, Melissa. (2001). *The Truth is. . . My Life, Love and Music*. Villard.

Fogelson, Genia. (1980). Belafonte. Holloway House.

Fisher, Eddie. (1981). *Eddie: My Life, My Loves*. Berkley Books.

Freeman, Bud .1989. *Crazeology: The Autobiography of a Chicago Jazzman*. University of Illinois Press.

Goldman, Herbert, 1988. *Jolson: The Legend Comes to Life*. Oxford Univ. Press.

_____ 1992. *Fannie Brice: The Original Funny Girl*. Oxford Univ. Press.

Goldrosen, John.1975. *The Buddy Holly Story*. Bowling Green Univ. Press.

Gottfried, Martin.1996. George *Burns: The Hundred Year Dash*. Simon & Schuster.

Gourse, Leslie.1991. *Unforgettable: The Life and Mystique of Nat King Cole*. St. Martin's Press.

Gresham, William. 1959. *Harry Houdini: The Man Who Walked Through Walls*. McFadden.

Gubernick, Lisa.1993. *Trisha Yearwood: Get Hot or Go Home*. Wm. Morrow.

Hall, Ward.1981. *The Struggles and Triumphs of a Modern Day Showman*. Sarasota: Carnival Publs.

Hasse, John.1993. *The Life and Genius of Duke Ellington*. Simon & Schuster.

Hawes, Hampton.1974. *A Portrait of Hampton Hawes: Raise Up Off of Me*. De Capo Press.

Henner, Marilu.1994. *Marilu Henner: By All Means Keep On Moving*. Pocket Books.

Hodes, Art.1992. *Hot Man. The Life of Al Hodes*. University of Illinois Press.

Hopkins, Jerry and Danny Sugerman. 1980. *No One Here Gets Out Alive*. Warner Books.

Hotchner, A. E. 1975. *Doris Day: Her Own Story*. Bantam.

Ivory, Steven.1985. *Tina*. Praeger.

James, Etta. 1995. *Rage to Survive*. Villard Books.

Jennings, Waylon.1996. *Waylon: An Autobiography*. Warner Books.

Jones, George.1996. *George Jones: I Lived to Tell it All*. Villard.

Jones, Margaret.1994. *Patsy: The Life and Times of Patsy Cline*. Harper Collins.

Josefsberg, Milt.1977. *The Jack Benny Show: The Life and Times of America's Best-Loved Entertainer*. Arlington House.

Kanelman, Martin. 1999. *Jim Carrey: The Joker is Wild*. Firefly Books: Pergamon.

Keller, Keith.1989. *Oh, Jess! A Jazz Life*. Magan Music Corp.

Khair, Emille. 1997. *Passion's Piano: The Eddie Heywood Story*. Care Publ. House.

King, B. B.1999. Blues *All Around Me: The Autobiography of B. B. King*. Avon Books.

Kinison, Bill.1994. *Brother Sam: The Short, Spectacular Life of Sam Kinison*. William Morrow

Kirely, Ed.1975. *'Ain't Misbehavin': The Story of Fats Waller*. De Capo Press.

Klein, Joe .1980. *Woody Guthrie: A Life*. Alfred Knopf.

LaBelle Patti.1996. *Don't Block the Blessings: Revelations of a Lifetime*. Riverhead Books, Putnam.

Latifah, Queen. 1999. *Ladies First: Revelations of a Strong Woman*. Wm. Morrow.

Lawrence, Carol. 1990. *Carol Lawrence: The Backstage Story*. McGraw Hill.

Lewis, Jerry. 1982. *Jerry Lewis in Person*. Pinnacle Books.

Lewis, Myra.1982. *Great Balls of Fire: The Uncensored Life of Jerry Lee Lewis*. Quill.

Liberace. 1973. *Liberace: An Autobiography*. G. P. Putnam.

Light, Alan.1977. *Tupac Shakur: 1971-1996*. Random House.

Love, Darlene.1998. *My Name is Love: The Darlene Love Story*. Wm. Morrow.

Lynn, Loretta. 1976. *Coal Miner's Daughter*. Warner Books.

Mandrell, Barbara.1990. *Get To the Heart: My Story*. Bantam Books.

Marsh, David.1979. *Born to Run: The Bruce Springsteen Story*. Dell Books.

Marx, Arthur.1979. *Red Skelton: An Unauthorized Biography*. E. P. Dutton.

Marx, Maxine.1980. *Growing Up with Chico*. Prentice Hall.

Mattson, Heidi.1995. *Ivy League Stripper*. St. Martin's Press

McCabe, John.1966. *An Affectionate Biography of Laurel and Hardy*. Doubleday.

McCall, Michael.1999. *Garth Brooks*. Barham.

McEntire, Reba. 1992. *Reba: My Story*. Bantam.

Merman, Ethel.1978. *Merman*. Simon & Schuster.

Miller, Norma.1996. *Swingin' At the Savoy: the Memoir of a Jazz Dancer*. Temple Univ. Press.

Minch, Stephen. 1992. *A Life Among Secrets: The Uncommon Life of Eddie Fields*. Hermetic Press.

Monti, Carla.1973. *W. C. Fields and Me*. Warner.

Nelson, Willie. 1988. *Willie: An Autobiography*. Pocket Books.

Newman, Phyllis. 1988. *Just In Time: Notes from My Life*. Simon & Schuster.

Nicholson, Stuart.1995. *Billie Holiday*. Northeastern Univ. Press.

Nickson, Chris.1998. Mariah *Carey: Her Story*. St. Martin's Press.

Phillips, John.1986. *Papa John*. Dell.

Porterfield, Nolan.1979. *Jimmie Rogers: The Life and Times of America's Blue Yodeler*. University of Illinois Press.

Pruetzel, Maria. 1978. *The Freddie Prinze Story*. Masters Press.

Pugh, Ronnie.1999. *Ernest Tubb: The Texas Troubadour*. Duke Univ. Press.

Radner, Gilda.1984. *It's Always Something*. Avon.

Rapp, Augustus.1959. *The Life and Times of Augustus Rapp*. Ireland Publ. Co.

Rivers, Joan.1986. *Enter Talking*. Delacorte Press.

Robbins, Jhan.1991. *Inka, Dinka, Doo: The Life of Jimmie Durante*. Paragon House.

Rose, Al.1979. *Eubie Blake*. MacMillan Publ.

Rose, Jim.1995. *Freak Like Me: Inside the Circus Sideshow*. Dell Books.

Schacter, James.1975. *Piano Man: The Story of Ralph Sutton*. Jaynor Press.

Siegel, Dorothy.1982. *The Glory Road: The Story of Josh White*. Shoe Tree Press.

Sothern, Georgia.1972. *My Life in Burlesque*. Signet Books.

Sparks, Kriston. 1991. *Ricky Martin: Livin' the Crazy Life*. Berkley Books.

Starr, Hedy Jo.1965. *My Unique Change*. Novel Books.

Stebbins, Jon (no publ. date given) *Dennis Wilson: The Real Beach Boy*. ECW Press.

Storm, Tempest.1987. *Tempest Storm: The Last Superstar of Burlesque*. Peachtree Publs

Taraborrelli, Randy.1991. *Michael Jackson: Magic and Madness*. Carol Publ. Co.

Taylor, Robert.1989. *Fred Allen: His Life and Wit*. Little Brown and Co.

Thomas, Bob.1984. *Astaire: The Man The Dancer*. St. Martin's Press.

Thurston, Howard and Jane Thurston. 1989. *Our Life in Magic*. Temple Publ.

Tillis, Mel.1984. *Stutterin' Boy*. Dell.

Townsend, Charles.1976. *San Antonio Rose: The Life and Music of Bob Wills*. University of Illinois Press.

Tritt, Travis.1994. *Ten Feet Tall and Bulletproof*. Warner Books.

Vagoda, Ben. 1993. *Will Rogers: A Biography*. Alfred Knopf.

Vallee, Rudy.1962. *My Time is Your Time: The Rudy Vallee Story*. Ivan Obolensky, Inc.

Williams, Jett.1990. Ain't *Nothin' As Sweet as my Baby: The Story of Hank Williams' Lost Daughter*. Berkley Books.

William, Gunther-Gebel. 1991. *Untamed: The Autobiography of the Circus' Greatest Animal Trainer*. Wm. Morrow & Co.

Williams, John, and Dennis Williams. 1993. *If I Stop I'll Die: The Comedy and Tragedy of Richard Pryor*. Thunder's Mouth Press.

Williams, Roger. 1973. *Sing a Sad Song: The Life of Hank Williams*. Ballantine Books.

Winer, Deborah. 1996. *The Night and the Music: Rosemary Clooney, Barbara Cook, Julie Wilson: Inside the World of Cabaret*. Simon & Schuster.

Wiseman, Rich. 1987. *Neil Diamond: Solitary Star*. Dodd Mead.

Wolff, Daniel.1995. *You Send Me: The Life and Times of Sam Cooke*. Wm. Morrow.

Wynette, Tammy. 1979. *Stand By Your Man*. Pocket Books.

Young, Steven. 1984. *Prince*. Perigee Books.

BIBLIOGRAPHY

Alper, N., G. Wassall, J. Feffrie, R. Greenblat, A. Kay, et al. 1996. *Artists in the Workforce: Employment and Earnings, 1970-1990*. National Endowment for the Arts: Seven Locks Press.

Als, Hilton. 1999. "A Pryor Love: The Life and Times of America's Comic Prophet of Race." *New Yorker*, Sept.13:68-81.

Ames, David. 1973. "A Sociocultural View of Hausa Musical Activity," Pp. 128-161 in *The Traditional Artist in African Societies* edited by Warren d'Azevedo. Indiana University Press.

Aptekar, Lewis. 1991. "Are Columbian Street Children Neglected? The Contributions of Ethnographic and Ethnohistorical Approaches to the Study of Children," *Anthropology and Education Quarterly*, 22:326-349.

Appignanesi, Lisa. 1975. *The Cabaret*. Cassell & Collier MacMillan Publ.

Ashihara, Eiryo. 1965. *The Japanese Dance*. Japan Travel Bureau.

Baddeley, V. C. 1952. *The Burlesque Tradition in the English Theatre after 1600*. Methuen & Co.Ltd.

Barish, Jonas. 1985. *The Antitheatrical Prejudice*. University of California Press.

Barr, Hamet, Robert Langs, Robert Holt, Leo Goldberger George Klein. 1972. *LSD: Personality and Experience*. Wiley.

Bauman, Richard. 1984. *Verbal Art as Performance*. Waveland Press.

Bayton, Mavis. 1999. *Frock Rock: Women Performing Popular Music*. Oxford University Press.

Bean, Annemarie, James Hatch, Brooks McNamara. 1996. *Inside the Minstrel Mask: Readings in Nineteenth Century Blackface Minstrelsy*. Wesleyan University Press.

Becker, Howard. 1951. "The Professional Dance Musician and His Audience," *American Journal of Sociology* 57:136-144.

Bennett, H. Stith. 1980. *On Becoming a Rock Musician*. University of Mass.

Berland, Joseph. 1982. *No Five Fingers are Alike: Cognitive Amplifiers in a Social Context*. Harvard University Press.

Berliner, Paul. 1978. *The Soul of 'Mbira': Music and Tradition of the Shona People of Zimbabwe*. University of California Press.

Berndt, Ronald and Catherine Berndt. 1964. *The World of the First Australians: An Introduction to the Traditional Life of Australian Aborigines*. University of Chicago Press.

Betelille, Andre. 1965. *Caste, Class and Power: Changing Patterns of Stratification in a Tanjore Village*. University of California Press.

Bielby, William and Denise Bielby. 1999. "Organization of Project-Based Labor Markets: Talent Agencies and the Careers of Screenwriters." *American Sociological Review* 64:64-85.

Blacking, John. 1995. *Music, Culture and Experience: Selected Papers of John Blacking*. University of Chicago Press.

Bloland, Sue. 1999. "Fame: The Power and Cost of a Fantasy." *The Atlantic Monthly*, November: 51-62.

Bogdan, Robert. 1988. *Freak Show: Presenting Human Oddities for Amusement and Profit*. University of Chicago Press.

Boles, Don. 1968. "Some Gypsy Occupations in America," *Journal of the Gypsy Lore Society*, 38:103-110.

Boles, Jacqueline. 1974. *Stripping for a Living: An Occupational Study of Nightclub Strippers*. Unpub. Diss. University of Georgia.

_____, and Albeno Garbin.1974a. "The Choice of Stripping for a Living: An Empirical and Theoretical Exploration." *Sociology of Work and Occupations* 1:110-123.

_____1974b "The Strip Club and Stripper Customers Patterns of Interaction," *Sociology and Social Research* 58:136-144.

_____2005. "Mental as Anything," Shocked *and Amazed* 8:49-51.

Bourdieu, Pierre. 1984. *Distinction: A Social Critique of the Judgment of Taste*. Harvard University Press.

Bowers, Faubion. 1953. *The Dance in India*. Columbia University Press.

Branson, L. H. no date given. *Magic of India*. (Original title Indian Conjuring) republished Pinchpenny Press, 1973.

Brewster, Zachary 2003. "Behavioral and Interactional Patterns of Strip

Club Patrons: Tipping, Techniques, and Club Attendance," *Deviant Behavior* 24:221-243.

Brown, Junius. 1940. *The Psychodynamics of Abnormal Behavior.* McGraw Hill.

Burger, Eugene, Neale, Robert. 1995. *Magic and Meaning.* Hermetic Press.

Burns, George. *All My Best Friends.* G. P. Putnam's Sons. 1989.

Campbell, Colin. 1996. "On the Concept of Motive in Sociology." *Sociology* 30:101-114.

Carmelli, Yoram. 1991. "Performance and Family in the World of British Circus," *Semiotica* 85:257-289.

Caves, Richard. 2000. *Creative Industries: Contracts Between Art and Commerce.* Harvard Univ. Press.

Chance, Michael and Ray Larsen (Eds.) 1976. *The Social Structure of Attention.* Wiley.

Chyatte, Conrad. 1940. "Professional Traits of Professional Actors." *Occupations* 27:245-250.

Clarke, Gerald. 2000. *Get Happy.* Random House.

Corio, Ann. 1968. *This Was Burlesque.* Grossett & Dunlap.

Dabbs, James, Denise de LaRue, Paula Williams. 1990. "Testosterone and Occupational Choice: Actors, Ministers, and Other Men." *Journal of Personality and Social Psychology* 59:1261- 1265.

_____and Mary Dabbs. 2000. *Heroes, Rogues and Lovers: Testosterone and Behavior.* McGraw Hill.

Dahl, Linda. 1984. *Stormy Weather: The Music and Lives of a Century of Jazz Women.* Pantheon.

Davis, Tracy. 1991. *Actresses as Working Women: Their Social Identity in Victorian Culture.* Routledge.

Davison, Natasha. 1989. "Artist or Entertainer: The Professional Ideology of Musical Theatre Performers and Its Significance in Performance," Unpub. Georgia State Univ.

DeCordova, Richard. 1991. "The Emergence of the Star System in America." Pp. 17-29 in *Stardom: Industry of Desire* edited by Christine Gledhill. Routledge.

Denisoff, R. Serge and John Bridges. 1982. "Popular Music: Who are the Recording Artists?" *Journal of Communication* 32:132-142.

Derber, Charles. 1981. *The Pursuit of Attention: Power and Individualism in Everyday Life.* G. K. Hall & Co.

Dressel, Paula and David Petersen. 1982. "Gender Roles, Sexuality, and the Male Strip Show: The Structuring of Sexual Opportunity," *Sociological Focus* 15:151-62.

Dube, S. C. 1955. *Indian Village.* Routledge and Kegan Paul.

Dubois, J. A. 1928. Hindu Manners, Customs and Ceremonies. Clarendon Press.Dumont, Louis. 1970. *Homo Hierarchicus: The Caste System and Its Implications.* University of Chicago Press.

Easto, Patrick and Marcello Truzzi. 1974. "The Carnival as a Marginally Legal Work Activity: A Typological Approach to Work Systems." Pp.336-353 in *Deviant Behavior: Occupational and Organizational Bases* edited by Clifton Bryant. Rand McNally.

Enck, Graves and James Preston. 1988. "Counterfeit Intimacy: A Dramaturgical Analysis of an Erotic Performance," *Deviant Behavior* 9:369-81.

Ennis, Philip. 1993. "Back to Basics: The Diamond, The Stream and the Parade," *Culture* 8(1):15- 18.

Evans, Randolph, Richard Evans, Scott Carvajal, Susan Perry. 1996. "A Survey of Injuries among Broadway Performers," *American Journal of Public Health* 86:77-80.

Faulkner, Robert and Andy Anderson. 1987. "Short-term and Emergent Careers: Evidence from Hollywood." *American Journal of Sociology* 92:879-909.

Feiler, Bruce. 1999. "It's Garth Brooks, Bad Boy." *Atlanta Journal and Constitution,* September 26, L 3.

Fenichel, O. 1946. "On Acting." *Psychoanalytic Quarterly* 15:44-160.

Fernandez, James. 1973. "The Exposition and Imposition of Order: Artistic Expression in Fang Culture. Pp. 194-200 in *The Traditional Artist in African Societies* edited byWarren d'Azevdo. Indiana University Press.

Fiedler, Leslie. 1978. *Freaks, Myths and Images of the Secret Self.* Simon & Schuster.

Fisher, Seymour and Rhonda Fisher. 1981. *The World is Funny and Forever: A Psychological Analysis of Comedians, Clowns and Actors.* Lawrence Eribaum Assocs.

Fisher, W. 1984. "Narration as a Human Communication Paradigm: The Case of Moral Public Argument." *Communications Monographs* 51:1-22.

Florida, Richard. 2002. *The Rise of the Creative Class and How It is Transforming Work, Leisure, Community and Everyday Life.* Basic Books.

Fox, Ted 1983. *Showtime at the Apollo.* Holt.

Frederickson, Jon and James Rooney. 1988. "The Free-lance Musician as a Type of Non-person: An Extension of the Concept of Non-personhood." *The Sociological Quarterly* 29:221-239.

Freidson, Eliot. 2001. *Professionalism: the 3rd Logic.* University of Chicago Press.

Friedlander, Paul. 1996. *Rock and Roll: A Social History.* Westview Press.

Friedman, Norman. 1990. "The Hollywood Actor: Occupational Culture, Career, and Adaptation to a Buyer's Market Industry." *Current Research on Occupations and the Professions* 5: 73-89.

Friedson, Steven. 1996. *Dancing Prophets: Musical Experience in Tumbuka Healing.* University of Chicago Press.

Gans, Herbert. 1974. *Popular Culture and High Culture.* Basic Books.

Garofalo, Reebee. 1997. *Rockin' Out: Popular Music in the USA.* Allyn & Bacon.

Gernet, Jacque. 1962. *Daily Life in China on the Eve of the Mongol Invasion,* 1250-1276. MacMillan.

Giuffre, Katherine. 1999. "Sandpiles of Opportunity: Success in the Art World." *Social Forces* 77:815-32.

Ginzberg, Eli et al. 1953. *Occupational Choice: An Approach to a General Theory.* Columbia University Press.

Gledhill, Christine. 1991. *Stardom: Industry of Desire.* Routledge.

Gmelch, Sharon. 1986. "Groups that Don't Want In: Gypsies and Other Artisan, Trader, and Entertainer Minorities" *Annual Review of Anthropology* 15:307-30.

Goldner, June. 1983. "The Early History and Development of the Solo Vocalist: Social Stress in Singing," pp. 150-165 in Jack Kamerman and Rosanne Martorella (Eds.) *Performers and Performances: The Social Organization of Artistic Work.* J. F. Bergin, Publs.

Green, Richard and John Money. 1996. "Stage Acting, Role Taking and Effeminate Impersonation." *Archives of General Psychiatry* 15:535-538.

Greenbaum, Andrea. 1997. "Women Comic Voices: The Art and Craft of Female Humor," *American Studies* 38:117-138.

Groce, Stephen, Margaret Cooper, 1990. "Just Me and the Boys? Women in Local-Level Rock and Roll," *Gender and Society* 4:220-229.

Hanks, D. 1986. "'Quike Bookis'--The Corpus Christi Drama and English Children in the Middle Ages, "Pp.118-127 in *Popular Culture in the Middle Ages* edited by Josie Campbell. Bowling Green State University Popular Press.

Hanners, John 1993. *"It Was Play or Starve": Acting in the Nineteenth-Century American Popular Theatre.* Bowling Green State University Popular Press.

Harwood, Ronald. 1984. *All the World's a Stage.* Little Brown & Co.

Hesmondhalgh, David. 1998. "The British Dance Music Industry: a Case Study of Independent Cultural Production," *British Journal of Sociology* 49:234-254.

_____2002. *The Cultural Industries.* London: Sage.

Holland, John. 1973. *Making Vocational Choices: A Theory of Careers.* Prentice Hall.

Hopper, DeWolf. 1927. Once *a Clown, Always a Clown.* Little, Brown & Co.

Janus, Samuel. 1980. "The Great Jewish-American Comedians' Identity Crisis," *The American Journal of Psychoanalysis* XL: 259-265.

Jones, J. 1989. "A Sociohistorical Perspective on Tunisian Women as Professional Musicians." Pp. 69-83 in *Women and Music in a Cross-cultural Perspective* edited by Ellen Koskoff. Greenwood Press.

Kasule, Samuel. 1998. "Popular Performance and the Construction of Social Reality in Post-Amin Uganda," *Journal of Popular Culture,* 32:39-58.

Kaplan, James. 2000. "The Laughing Game." *New Yorker* 252-663.

Keyes, Cheryl. 1991. "We're More than a Novelty, Boys: Strategies of Female Rappers in the Rap Music Tradition," in Joan Radner (Ed.) Feminist Messages: *Coding in Women's Folk Culture.* Univ. of Illinois Press.

Kirby, E. T. 1975. *Ur-Drama: The Origins of Theatre.* New York University Press.

Koskoff, Ellen. 1987. "An Introduction to Women, Music and Culture." Pp. 1-23 in *Women, and Music in a Cross-cultural Perspective* edited by Ellen Koskoff. Greenwood Press.

Krickenberg, Dieter. 1983. "On the Social Status of the Spielmann ('Folk Musician') in the 17th Century Germany, Particularly in the Northwest." Pp. 95-122 in *The Social Status of the Professional Musician from the Middle Ages to the 19th Century* (annotated and translated from the German by Herbert Kaufman and Barbara Reisner), edited by Walter Salem in *The Sociology of Music*, No. 1. Pendragon Press.

Lane, Yoti. 1960. *The Psychology of the Actor.* The John Day Co.

Lenski, Gerhard. 1966. *Power and Privilege.* McGraw Hill.

Lerner, Robert, Althea Nagai, Stanley Rothman. 1996. *American Elites.* Yale University Press.

Levine, Lawrence. 1988. *Lowbrow/Highbrow: The Emergence of a Cultural Hierarchy in America.* Harvard University Press.

Lewis, Lisa. (Ed.). 1992. *The Adoring Audience: Fan Culture and Popular Media.* Routledge.

Lhamon, W. T. 1996. "Ebery Time I Weel About I Jump Jim Crow: Cycles of Minstrel Transgression from Cool White to Vanilla Ice," pp. 275-284 in Annemarie Bean, James Hatch, Brooks McNamara (Eds.*) Inside the Minstrel Mask: Readings in Nineteenth Century Minstrelsy.* University Press of New England.

Linde, Debbie. 1992. "Sawdust in Their Shoes: Black Performers in American Circuses," *American Visions* 7:12-19.

Little, W. Kenneth. 1991. "The Rhetoric of Romance and the Simulation of Tradition in the Circus Clown Performance," *Semiotica* 85:227-255.

Lommel, Andreas. 1967. *Shamanism: The Beginning of Art.* McGraw Hill.

Lott, Eric. 1993. *Love and Theft: Blackface Minstrelsy and the American Working Class.* Oxford University Press.

Luck, Georg. 1986. *Arcana Mundi: Magic and the Occult in Greek and Roman Worlds.* John Hopkins University Press.

Mahar, William. 1998. *Behind the Burnt Cork Mask: Early Blackface Minstrelsy and the Antebellum American Popular Culture.* University of Pennsylvania Press.

McAdams, Dan. 1982. "Experiences of Intimacy and Power: Relationships Between Social Motives and Autobiographical Memory," *Journal of Personality and Social Psychology* 42:292-302.

McClelland, David. 1985. *Human Motivation.* Scott Foresman.

Malcolmson, Robert. 1973. *Popular Recreations in English Society, 1700-1850.* Cambridge University Press.

MacLeod, Bruce. 1993. *Club Date Musicians: Playing the New York Party Circuit.* University of Illinois Press.

McArthur, Benjamin. 1984. *Actors and American Culture, 1880-1920.* Temple University Press.

Malinowski, Bronislaw. 1925. "Complex and Myth in Mother-right." *Psyche*: 194-216.

Mann, Charles. 2000. "The Heavenly Jukebox." *The Atlantic Monthly*, September: 29-59.

Matlaw, Myron. 1967. *The Black Crook and Other Nineteenth Century American Plays.* E. P. Dutton & Co.

Marx, Harpo. 1961. *Harpo Speaks.* Bernard Geis Assocs.

Mayhew, Henry. 1968. *London Labour and London Poor, Vol. III.* Dover Press.

Menger, Pierre-Michel. 1999. "Artistic Labor Markets and Careers." *Annual Review of Sociology* 25:541-74.

Merriam, Alan. 1964. *The Anthropology of Music.* Northwestern University Press.

Mills, C. Wright. 1940. "Situated Action and the Vocabulary of Motives." *American Sociological Review* 5:904-13.

Mintz, Lawrence. 1985. "Standup Comedy as Social and Cultural Mediation." *American Quarterly* 37:71-79.

Mullen, Ken. 1985. "Impure Performance Frame of the Public House Entertainer," *Urban Life* 14:181-203.

Nardi, Peter. 1988. "The Social World of Magicians: Gender and Conjuring," *Sex Roles* 19:759-770.

National Endowment of the Arts. 1976. *Employment and Unemployment of Artists: 1970-1975.* Research Report No 1.

Newton, Esther. 1972. *Mother Camp: Female Impersonators in America.* University of Chicago Press.

Neuringer, Charles. 1989. "On the Question of Homosexuality in Actors." *Archives of Sexual Behavior* 18:523-529.

Noell, Mae. 1977. "Recollections of Medicine Show Life." Pp. 215-226 in *American Popular Entertainments: Papers and Proceedings of the Conference on the History of American Popular Entertainment* edited by Myron Matlaw. Greenview Press.

O'Meally, Robert. 1991. *The Many Faces of Billie Holiday*. De Capio Press.

Passman, Arnold. 1971. *The Deejays*. The MacMillan Co.

Prehn, John. 1983. "Invasion of the Male Strippers: Realignment in a Small Town Strip Club," *Journal of Popular Culture* 17: 183-186.

Psvletich, Aida. 1980. *Sirens of Song: The Popular Female Vocalist in America*. De Capo.

Petersen, David and Paula Dressel. 1982. "Equal Time for Women: Social Notes on the Male Strip Show," *Urban Life* 11:185-208.

Perruci, Alissa. 2000. "The Relationship between Persona and Self in Exotic Dancers," *Current Research on Occupations and the Professions* 11:35-53.

Peterson, Richard. 1994. "Cultural Studies Through the Production Perspective,"Pp. 163-89 in *The Sociology of Culture* edited by Diane Crane. Blackwell.

_____1982. "Five Constraints on the Production of Culture: Law, Technology, Market, Organizational Structure and Occupational Careers," *Journal of Popular Culture* 16:143-153.

Petzoldt, R. 1983. "The Economic Conditions of the 18th Century Musician."Pp. 161-188 in The Social Status of the Professional Musician from the Middle Ages to the 19th Century. (Annotated and translated by Herbert Kaufman and Barbara Reisner) edited by Walter Salem in *Sociology of Music, No. 1*. Pergamon Press.

Post, Jennifer. "Professional Women in Indian Music: The Death of the Courtesan," Pp. 97-109 in *Women and Music in Cross-Cultural Perspective* edited by Ellen Koskoff. Greenwood Press.

Price, J. 1968. "The Economic Organization of Outcastes." *Anthropological Quarterly* 41: 209-217.

Prus, Robert, Styllianoss Irini. 1980. Hookers, *Rounders and Desk Clerks*. Sage.

Ronai, Carol and Carolyn Ellis. 1989. "Turn-Ons for Money:

Interactional Strategies of the Table Dancer." *Journal of Contemporary Ethnography*, 18:271-298.

Ronai, Carol and Cross, Rebecca 1998. "Dancing with Identity::Narrative Resistance Strategies of the Table Dancer, *"Journal of Contemporary Ethnography* 18:271-98.

Ronai, Carol. 1992. "Managing Aging in Young Adulthood: The Aging Table Dancer," *Journal of Aging Studies* 6:307-317.

Roman, Paul and Terry Blum. 1982. "Alcohol, Pampering and the Rise to Social Stardom." *Contemporary Drug Problems* Summer: 223-242.

Rosen, Sherwin. 1986. "The Theory of Equalizing Differences." Pp. 641-692 in *Handbook of Labour Economics* edited by O. Ashenfelter and R. Layard: North-Holland.

Ruttenberg, Robert, W. Friedman, P. Kilgannon, W. Gutchess. 1982. *Working and Not Working in the Performing Arts*. A report prepared by Ruttenberg and associates for Equity, the American Federation of Radio Artists, American Guild of Musical Artists, Screen Actors Guild, and the American Federation of Musicians.

Salem, Walter. 1983. "The Social Status of Musicians in the Middle Ages."Pp. 3-29 in *The Social Status of the Professional Musician from the Middle Ages to the 19th Century*. (Annotated and translated by Herbert Kaufman and Barbara Reisner) edited by Walter Salem in *Sociology of Music, No. 1*. Pergamon Press.

Salutin, Marilyn. 1973. "The Impression Management Techniques of the Burlesque Comic." *Sociological Inquiry* 43:159-168.

_____1971. "Stripper Morality." *Transaction*. 8:391-405.

Sanderson, Michael. 1984. *From Irving to Olivier: A Social History of the Acting Profession in England, 1880-1983*. St. Martin's Press.

Schechner, Richard. 1985. *Between Theater and Anthropology*. University of Pennsylvania Press.

Schickel, Richard. 1985. *Intimate Strangers: The Culture of Celebrity*. Doubldeday.

Shaw, Artie. 1999. "Reaping the Whirlwind," *Newsweek*. June 28:30.

Shively, D. 1968. "Bakefu vs. Kabuki." Pp. 231-261 in *Studies in the Institutional History of Early Modern Japan* edited by John Hall and Marius Jansen. Princeton.

Shrum, Wesley. 1996. Fringe *and Fortune: The Role of the Critic in High and Popular Art*. Princeton University Press.

Shumaker, Wayne. 1954. *English Autobiography: Its Emergence, Materials and Form*. University of California Press.

Simmel, Georg. 1971. *On Individuality and Social Fo*rms edited by D. Levine. University of Chicago Press.

Skipper, James and Charles McCaghy. 1971. "Stripteasing: A Sex Oriented Occupation." Pp.275- 296 in *Studies in the Sociology of Sex* edited by James Henslin. Appleton-Century Crofts.

Spitzer, M. 1984. "The Mechanics of Vaudeville." Pp. 167-178 in *American Vaudeville as Seen by Its Contemporaries* edited by Charles Stein: Alfred Knopf.

Stebbins, Robert. 1990. The Laugh-Makers: Stand-up Comedy as *Art, Business and Life-Style*. McGill Queen's University Press.

_____1992. Amateurs, *Professionals and Serious Leisure*. McGill Queen's University Press.

_____1984. *The Magician: Career, Culture, and Social Psychology in a Variety Art*. Clarke Irwin.

Stein, Charles (Ed.) 1984. *American Vaudeville as Seen By Its Contemporaries*. Alfred Knopf.

Sugarman, Robert. 2002. "Circus in the Global Economy," Paper presented at the annual meeting of the Popular Culture Association, April 20.

Sutherland, Anne. 1975. *The Hidden Americans*. Free Press.

Sutton, A. 1987. "Identity and Individuality in an Ensemble Tradition: The Female Vocalist in Java." Pp. 111-130 in *Women and Music in a Cross-cultural Perspective* edited by Ellen Koskoff. Greenwood Press.

Seabrook, John. 2003. "The Money Note," *The New Yorker*, July7:42-55.

Strauss, Anselm, Juliet Corbin. 1998. *Basics of Qualitative Research; Techniques and Procedures for Developing Grounded Theory. 2nd Ed.* Sage.

Stuart, Andrea. 1996. *Showgirls*. Jonathan Cape.

Sway, Marilyn. 1988. *Familiar Strangers: Gypsy Life in America*. University of Illinois Press.

Taft, Ronald. 1961. "Psychological Assessment of Professional Actors and Related Professions." *Genetic Psychological Monographs* 64:309-383.

Tewksbury, Richard. 1993. "Men Performing as Women: Explorations in the World of Female Impersonation." *Sociological Spectrum* 13:465-486.

_____1994. "A Dramaturgical Analysis of Male Strippers," *The Journal of Men's Studies* 2:325-42.

Thayer, Lee. 1986. "On the Mass Media and Mass Communication: Notes Toward a Theory."Pp. 41-61 in *Inter/media: Interpersonal Communication in a Media World, 3rd Edition* edited by Gary Gumpert and Robert Cathcart: Oxford University Press.

Thomas, W. I. 1969. *The Unadjusted Girl.* Patterson Smith.

Thompson, William, Jackie Harred. 1992. "Topless Dancers: Managing Stigma in a Deviant Occupation," *Deviant Behavior* 13:291-311.

Toll, Robert. 1977. "Showbiz in Blackface: The Evolution of the Minstrel Showas a Theatrical Form." Pp. 21-32 in *American Popular Entertainment: Papers and Proceedings of the Conference on the History of American Popular Entertainment* edited by Myron Matlaw: Greenview Press.

_____1982. *The Entertainment Machine: American Show Business in the Twentieth Century.* Oxford University Press.

Truzzi, Marcello. 1968. "The Decline of the American Circus: The Shrinkage of an Institution." Pp. 314-322 in Sociology in Everyday Life edited by Marcello Truzzi: Prentice Hall.

Tucker, Sherrie. 1999. "The Prairie View Co-eds: Black College Female Musicians in Class and on the Road During WWII," *Black Music Research,* 19:93-126.

Valdez, Avelardo, Jeffrey Halley. 1996. "Gender in the Culture of Mexican-American Conjunto Music," *Gender & Society* 10:148-167.

Weber, Max. 1964. *The Theory of Social and Economic Organization.* The Free Press.

Wilmut, Roger. 1985. *Kindly Leave the Stage: The Story of Variety, 1919-1960.* Methun.

Watts, Isaac. 1926. "Against Idleness and Mischief," P. 57 in *The Oxford Book of 18th Century Verse* edited by D. Smith: Oxford University Press.

Welsford, Enid. 1935. *The Fool: His Social and Literary History*. Faber & Faber.

Wiersma, Jacquelyn. 1988. ": The Press Release: Symbolic Communication in Life History Interviewing," *Journal of Personality* 56:205-238.

Wilhelm, Sidney and Gideon Sjoberg 1958. "The Social Characteristics of Entertainers." *Social Forces* 38: 71-76.

Winter, David. 1988. "The Power Motive in Women---and Men." *Journal of Personality and Social Psychology* 54:510-519.

_____ and Abigail Stewart. 1978. "The Power Motive."Pp. 391-441 in *Dimensions of Personality* edited by H. London and J. Exner. Wiley.

_____and Leslie Carlson. 1988. "Using Motive Scores in the Psychobiographical Study of an Individual: The Case of Richard Nixon." *Journal of Personality* 56:75-103.

Wood, Elizabeth. 2000. "Working in the Fantasy Factory: The Attention Hypothesis and the Enacting of Masculine Power in Strip Clubs," *Journal of Contemporary Ethnography* 29:5- 27.

Yang, Chung-i. 1956. "Lower Caste in the T'ang Dynasty." Pp. 185-191 in *Chinese Social History: Translations of Selected Studies* edited by E-Tu Sun and John de Francis. American Council of Learned Societies.

Zarbreggan, Eileen. 2000. "Social Motives and Cognitive Power-Sex Associations: Predictions of Aggressive Sexual Behavior." *Journal of Personality and Social Psychology* 78:559-581.

Zeidman, Irving. 1967. *The American Burlesque Show*. Hawthorne Books.

Zguta, Russell. 1978. *Russian Minstrels; A History of the Skomorokhhi*. University of Pennsylvania Press.

INDEX

In alphabetical order by first name.